MOTHER GOOSE

*A Basic Pantomime
in Three Acts*

by
TRUDY WEST

SAMUEL FRENCH

LONDON
NEW YORK SYDNEY TORONTO HOLLYWOOD

Copyright © 1950 by Samuel French Ltd
All Rights Reserved

MOTHER GOOSE is fully protected under the copyright laws of the British Commonwealth, including Canada, the United States of America, and all other countries of the Copyright Union. All rights, including professional and amateur stage productions, recitation, lecturing, public reading, motion picture, radio broadcasting, television and the rights of translation into foreign languages are strictly reserved.

ISBN 978-0-573-06437-1

www.samuelfrench.co.uk
www.samuelfrench.com

FOR AMATEUR PRODUCTION ENQUIRIES

UNITED KINGDOM AND WORLD
EXCLUDING NORTH AMERICA
plays@samuelfrench.co.uk
020 7255 4302/01

Each title is subject to availability from Samuel French,
depending upon country of performance.

CAUTION: Professional and amateur producers are hereby warned that MOTHER GOOSE is subject to a licensing fee. Publication of this play does not imply availability for performance. Both amateurs and professionals considering a production are strongly advised to apply to the appropriate agent before starting rehearsals, advertising, or booking a theatre. A licensing fee must be paid whether the title is presented for charity or gain and whether or not admission is charged.

No one shall make any changes in this title for the purpose of production. No part of this book may be reproduced, stored in a retrieval system, or transmitted in any form, by any means, now known or yet to be invented, including mechanical, electronic, photocopying, recording, videotaping, or otherwise, without the prior written permission of the publisher. No one shall upload this title, or part of this title, to any social media websites.

The right of Trudy West to be identified as author of this work has been asserted in accordance with Section 77 of the Copyright, Designs and Patents Act 1988.

PREFACE.

Of all our national forms of entertainment, the Pantomime is perhaps the most traditional and shows least signs of waning popularity. The average "run" of the professional pantomime is certainly as long as ever, and for many years it has been a source of considerable enjoyment and profit among amateur societies.

It is for this latter field of activity that this series of "BASIC PANTOMIME" has been specially designed, both as regards the "scripts", the settings, and the general production problems which face every company in work of this type.

Apart from the time-honoured stories on which all our pantomimes are (and rightly) based, much of their success depends on topicality, local and current humour, and by no means least upon the songs and choruses of the time— even of the year.

With this in view, these "basic" pantomimes have been prepared, not as the final, unalterable show, but as *bases* upon which may be built the ultimate product according to the desires, and the resources, of the individual company.

The scripts follow, in each case, the traditional stories very strictly. Any major departure would be resented by the youngest—and the oldest ! —members of the audience. The dialogue is in modern prose, and prepared so that " cuts", additions, and the introduction of " local " or " topical " references may be effected with a minimum of difficulty.

Simplicity has been the prior aim also with regard to the settings, which are dealt with in detail in the " Production Notes " for each of the scripts. These contain suggestions for yet further simplification where the exigencies of the theatre are exceptionally limited, as well as indications of elaboration for those which are more fortunately placed.

Equal consideration has been given to the matter of Musical Numbers, Dances, etc. Those indicated represent what may be regarded as a reasonable minimum ; in fact, where resources are available, one or two extra numbers might be added with advantage. But the basic form which the pantomimes take render these additions quite easy to effect.

On the other hand, it will be found that, if desired, the pantomimes may be produced without alteration in any department despite the title of " BASIC " which has, for the foregoing reasons, been conferred upon them.

CHARACTERS :

MOTHER GOOSE.

JACK
JILL } (her children).

SIR JASPER JABBERWOCK (the Squire).

BILL BIFFEM
BERT BASHEM } (the Squire's Bailiffs).

PETER (a young ploughman).

BETTY (a goose-girl).

FAIRY SUNBEAM.

THE DEMON KING.

KING GANDER
QUEEN KARIN } (Rulers of the Land of Geese).

ERMYNTRUDE (the Golden Goose).

SAM (a young farm worker).

SUSIE (a village girl).

THE GOOSE CHAMBERLAIN.

SGT. GREGORY (of the Gandoliers).

GRACIE (Goose Lady-in-Waiting).

CHORUS *of Villagers, Milkmaid, Guests, Geese.*

BALLET *of Goslings, Demons and Spirits.*

SCENES.

ACT I.

SCENE 1. *Outside Mother Goose's Cottage.*

SCENE 2. *The Farmyard. (OR—as in Scene I.)*

SCENE 3. *In the Forest.*

ACT II.

SCENE 1. *Interior of Mother Goose's Castle.*

SCENE 2. *The Forest. (As in Act I.)*

SCENE 3. *Outside the Cottage. (As in Act I, Scene 1.)*

ACT III.

SCENE 1. *The Forest. (As in previous Acts.)*

SCENE 2. *The Land of Geese.*

SCENE 3. *Interior of Castle. (As in Act II, Scene 1.)*

NOTE ON THE MUSICAL NUMBERS.

(With lyrics.)

(The following traditional airs fit the lyrics supplied.)

No. 4. *(Air : "Autumn Song").*

No. 6. *(Air : "The Maypole").*

No. 21. *(Air : "Song of the Western Men").*

No. 9. *(Air : "A-Hunting We Will Go.")*

No. 13. *(Air : "Down Among the Dead Men.")*

No. 16. *(Air : "Begone, Dull Care.")*

No. 19. *(Air : "We're off to Philadelphia in the Morning.")*

No. 23. *(Air : "The British Grenadiers.")*

MUSICAL NUMBERS.

ACT I.

SCENE 1.

1. OPENING CHORUS   .. (VILLAGERS *and* MILKMAIDS)
2. DUET .. .. .. (JILL *and* PETER)
3. DUET .. .. .. (JACK *and* BETTY)
4. ENSEMBLE : *"An Egg a Day"* .. (THE COMPANY)

INTERLUDE.

5. SONG .. .. (MOTHER GOOSE *and* CHORUS)

SCENE 2.

6. SONG .. .. .. (JACK)
7. ENSEMBLE : *"Marketing Song"* .. (BETTY, SUSIE, SAM *and* CHORUS)
7a. REPRISE *Refrain of* No. 4 (MOTHER GOOSE, JACK *and* JILL)

INTERLUDE.

8. SONG .. .. .. (FAIRY SUNBEAM)

SCENE 3.

9. TRIO : *"Three Bouncing Buccaneers"* (SIR JASPER, BERT *and* BILL)

ACT II.

SCENE 1.

10. OPENING CHORUS   .. (THE GUESTS)
11. SONG .. .. .. (MOTHER GOOSE *and* CHORUS)
12. WALTZ SONG (*and* DANCE)   .. (THE COMPANY)

INTERLUDE.

13. DUET .. .. .. (BILL *and* BERT)

Scene 2.

14.   Ballet   ..   ..   (Demons)
15.   Quartette : " *I'd Rather Be . . .* " (Mother Goose,
                                Sir Jasper, Bill *and* Bert)

Interlude.

15a. Ballet   ..   ..   (Demons)

Scene 3.

16.   Song ..   ..   ..   (Susie *and* Chorus)
17.   Quintette : " *Oh, Where's Our Goose ?* " (Mother
                        Goose, Jill, Jack, Betty *and* Peter)
18.   Chorus   ..   ..   (Full Company)

ACT III.

Scene 1.

19.   Song ..   ..   ..   (Peter)
20.   Solo : " *Off to Philadelphia* " .. (Mother Goose)
21.   Song ..   ..   ..   (Mother Goose)
22.   Chorus of Farewell   (Sam, Susie *and* Villagers)

Interlude.

22a. Reprise *Refrain of* No. 19   ..   (Peter)

Scene 2.

23.   Chorus of Homage ..   (The Geese)
24.   Ballet   ..   ..   (The Goslings)
25.   Chorus : " *The Fighting Gandoliers* " .. (Bodyguard
                                                of Geese)

25a. Reprise *of* No. 25   ..   (Bodyguard)
26.   Chorus   ..   ..   (Full Company)

Scene 3.

27.   Chorus (*and* Dance)..   (Wedding Guests)
27a. Reprise *of* 27..   ..   (Wedding Guests
28.   Finale Chorus   ..   (Full Company)

PRODUCTION NOTES.

The staging of MOTHER GOOSE presents little difficulty. The number of settings is FIVE. One of these is used three times, and two are used twice. Cut-cloths and simple wings alone are needed, there being no interior "box sets" required. Furniture and properties are exceptionally simple and most of the "magical" effects are obtained by lighting. A rostrum at the back may remain throughout.

A running tab at about half stage depth is advisable.

SETTINGS :

ACT I. SCENE 1. OUTSIDE THE COTTAGE.

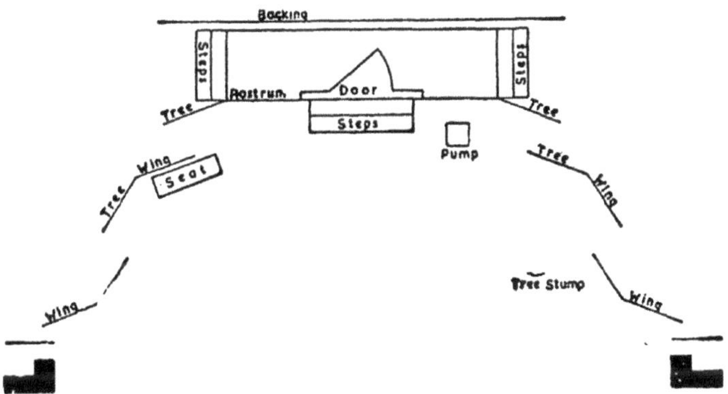

If desired, the cottage entrance may be up L., but the acting edition is marked for up C. It may be set in the central cut of a cut-cloth. A small seat, a tree stump, and if desired, a pump, are the only necessary furnishings. Tree wings mask in at each side.

SCENE 2.   THE FARMYARD.

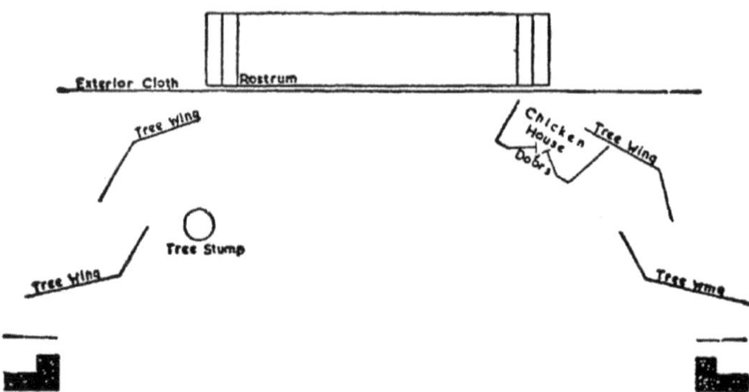

There is no reason why this scene should not be played on the setting for Scene 1. It is only suggested for variety. If the same setting is used, the chicken house should be set for both scenes.

If the "farmyard" setting is used, a back cloth, perhaps showing a wall and distant countryside, would be effective. Tree wings mask in as before.

INTERLUDE.

This may be played in front of the running tabs, or a front-cloth if more convenient.

SCENE 3.   THE FOREST.

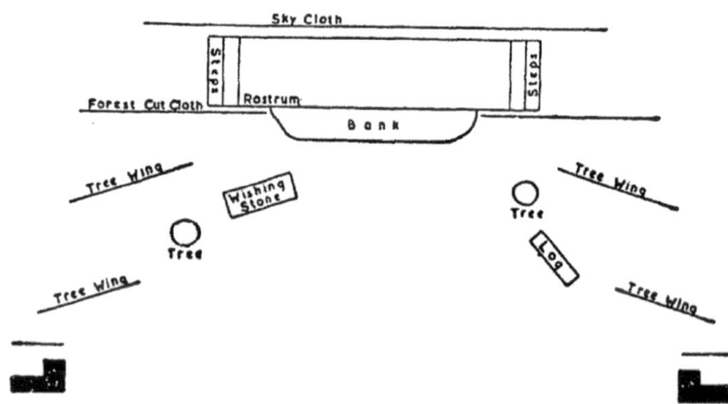

The rostrum should be disguised as a mossy bank, with either a ramp, or grass-covered steps down to stage level. If possible, the tree wings should be of gaunt and withered trees, with drooping, overhanging foliage. The Wishing Stone must be fairly solid. The log must bear the sitters' weights, but be light enough to raise by invisible wires or cords.

ACT II. SCENE 1. CASTLE INTERIOR.

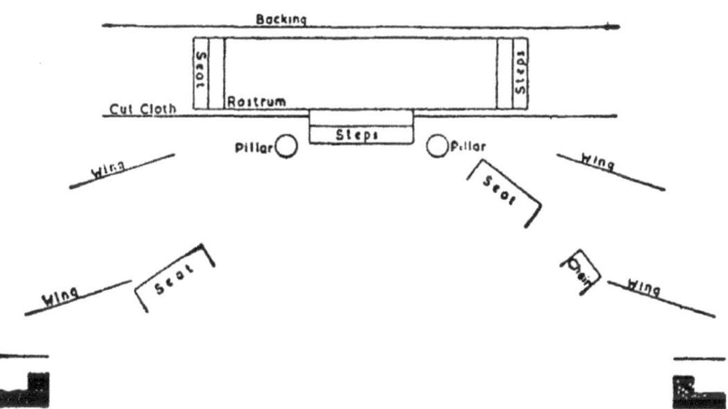

If a special interior cut-cloth and interior wings are NOT convenient, they can all be avoided by playing this scene in curtains. The curtain at the back will be open wide enough for a central entrance. The running tabs, closed slightly in, will help to mask, and other curtain wings set up stage may be employed as and when needed.

There should not be much furniture, and good wide exits should be provided, as in the other scenes, for effective entrances and exits of the Chorus. A vulgar, ornate, or even fantastic touch should be introduced into such furniture or decoration as may be decided upon.

SCENE 2.   (As in Act I, Sc. 3.)

SCENE 3.   (As in Act I, Sc. 1.)

(NOTE.—With regard to the above two scenes, if curtains and the running tabs are used for the Castle, the tree wings need not be struck, but remain hidden by curtains and tabs. This will save time and labour in setting.)

ACT III. SCENE 1. (As in Act 1, Sc. 3.)

INTERLUDE.

In front of tabs, or cloth.

SCENE 2. THE LAND OF GEESE.

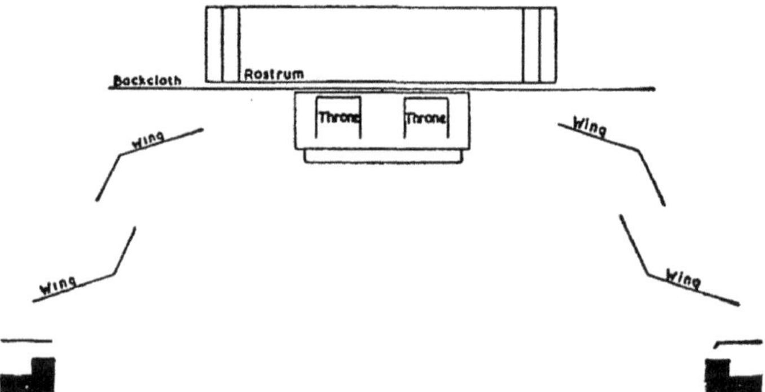

The Forest Scene for Scene 1 need NOT be struck during the "front of tabs" scene. A cloth may be lowered *in front of* the "mossy bank". It may be as described on the plan, or have any other simple design to suggest the scene. The "ice-wings" should be set if possible, or something equally simple.

The remainder of the Forest Scene may be struck during Scene 2.

SCENE 3. THE CASTLE INTERIOR.

This may be played in curtains, as before, if there is not the time, or the resources, to make the full change.

COSTUMES.

The only costumes requiring some thought and ingenuity are those for the GEESE.

ERMYNTRUDE should be disguised effectively as a goose, and the part may be played by a child.

The inhabitants of the Land of Geese should be in white, with sleeves and trousers tight around the wrists and ankles. Cardboard webbed feet should be attached to the ankles to rest on the top of the shoes. White bathing caps, or similar headgear, may be worn, and the faces made up white, with yellow noses and chins, if an especially realistic effect is desired.

The KING and QUEEN must have crowns—perhaps with feathers—and there should be something rather special or fantastic about their costumes. The CHAMBERLAIN, too, must be distinguished in some way. The GANDOLIERS might have military "pill-box" caps over their "bathing caps", and scarlet sashes, or a scarlet line down the seams of trousers.

MOTHER GOOSE*

ACT I.

SCENE I.

SCENE.—*A village green in Ptomania.*
Up C. *is the exterior of* MOTHER GOOSE'S *cottage, with a porch. There are one or two trees in the background and a rough wooden bench under one of them at* R.
(*See the* PRODUCTION NOTES.)

On the rise of the CURTAIN *a number of* VILLAGERS *are walking about arm-in-arm or "spooning" under the trees. A couple are on the seat gazing soulfully into each other's eyes. There is a background of " pastoral " music. A* CHORUS *of* MILKMAIDS *enters* R., *or up* C., *on their way to milking. They have pails on their arms.*

No. 1. OPENING CHORUS .. (VILLAGERS *and* MILKMAIDS)

(*This is followed by a* RUSTIC DANCE.)

(SUSIE *and* SAM *enter* R.)

SAM (*shouting excitedly*). Listen, everybody ! I've got some wonderful news for you.
ALL (*ad. lib.*). Oh ! What is it ? Do tell us quickly, Sam ! (*They crowd round* SAM *and* SUSIE.)
SAM (*drawing* SUSIE *forward*). Sue's just promised to marry me come Michaelmas. We're betrothed !

(SUSIE *wriggles and giggles in embarrassment.*)

ALL. Hooray ! Congratulations ! When's the wedding, Susie ? (*They re-group.*) You're a lucky lad, Sam ! (*Ad. lib.*)

(JILL *enters down* L. *She is a pretty little girl of about eighteen, dressed in poor, working garb.*)

---

* N.B. Paragraph 3 on page ii of this Acting Edition regarding photocopying and video-recording should be carefully read.

JILL.   Hullo, everybody.   What's all the excitement about ?

A MILKMAID.   Susie and Sam are engaged.   They're going to get married at Michaelmas, Jill !

JILL (*crossing to* C. *and kissing* SUSIE).   Oh, I'm so glad, Sue dear.   I *do* hope you and Sam will be very happy.

SUSIE.   Thank you, Jill.   But why don't you and Peter get engaged ?   I'd like to see you happy, too.

SAM.   Yes, why don't you, Jill ?   You're too pretty and too sweet not to be wed.

JILL (*sadly*).   Because Mother would never let us.   She seems to think an ordinary ploughman is not good enough for me.   Isn't she *awful* !

ALL.   Shame !

JILL (*looking round at them all*).   Peter is not ordinary at all—he's *quite* different !

SUSIE.   Of course he is !   (*Softly.*)   Everyone seems different when you're in love.

SAM.   Maybe she'll change her mind one day, Jill.

JILL.   Oh, I wish she would, but she's so *pig-headed !*

SAM (*looking off* R.).   Ah, here *is* Peter !   (*Winking and beckoning to the others.*)   Well, boys and girls, we'd better be getting back to work.   (*He indicates by gestures that they are to go out and leave* PETER *and* JILL *alone.*)   Two's company—so come along now !   (*The* CHORUS *move up stage.*)

(PETER *enters* R.   *He is a handsome young man, dressed in farmer's clothes, and whistling gaily.*)

(*The* CHORUS *begin to exit.*)

PETER (*to the departing chorus*).   What, going so soon ? I thought I heard some festive song.

SAM (*holding* SUSIE'S *hand*).   Aye, that's right, you did, Peter.   My Sue here has just promised to marry me, and the boys and girls were just congratulating of us, like.

PETER (*grasping their hands warmly*).   Then let me add *my* good wishes.   That's grand news, Sam.

SAM.   Thanks, Peter.   We were a-sayin' to Jill . . . (*He hesitates*).   Oh, well, we'd better be gettin' along ! (*To the* CHORUS.)   Come on, folks !

(*All exeunt, except* PETER *and* JILL.)

PETER (*crossing swiftly to* JILL *and taking her in his arms.*) Oh, how I wish it were us, Jill darling !

JILL (*sighing heavily*). So do I. It would be *heavenly* !

PETER. I wish Mother Goose could be brought to see reason. I shan't always be a ploughman. I shall work hard to buy a farm of my own some day, for you and me, Jill—just for you and me.

JILL. I know. I believe in you, Peter. To me, you're the most wonderful man in the world and it doesn't matter what else you are.

PETER (*very tenderly*). And you are the only girl for me.

No 2.   DUET   ..   ..   ..   (JILL *and* PETER)

(*After the Number they sit on the seat* R. *and indulge in a long embrace.* MOTHER GOOSE *enters from the cottage. She wears a voluminous blouse and skirt which shows an inch or two of red-stockinged leg above large, flat-heeled boots. Her hair is screwed into a bun on top of her head. She carries a broom on which she leans for a moment or two silently surveying the lovers, her whole attitude one of outraged surprise.*)

MOTHER GOOSE (*indignantly*). Well, chase me round the compost heap ! What's all this going on ? Break away, there, break away !

(PETER *and* JILL *hear the last phrase and spring to their feet guiltily.* MOTHER GOOSE *advances threateningly with her broom to* PETER, *who moves to* C.)

You lazy, good-for-nothing son of a never-mind-what ! Get back to your plough and leave my girl alone—go on, go on ! (*She "sweeps" him away with her broom.*)

PETER (*laughing as he retreats*). Oh, don't be angry, Mother Goose. We didn't mean any harm.

MOTHER GOOSE. You better 'adn't !

JILL (R. *of* PETER). Leave him alone, Mother. (*Suddenly, blurting it out.*) Peter and I love each other.

MOTHER GOOSE (*sarcastically*). Oh, is *that* what it was ? Thanks for telling me !

B

PETER (*quickly*). Yes, and we want to get married.

MOTHER GOOSE (*screaming it out*). *Married* ? Over my dead body—which makes it a funeral ! (*To* JILL.) When you marry, my girl, it's got to be somebody who goes up in the world—somebody like a liftman or a mountaineer.

PETER (*bitterly*). Or someone with money at the back of him, like the commissionaire of a Bank, I suppose.

MOTHER GOOSE. There's enough poverty in this family. Why, I haven't been able to pay the rent for weeks. Besides, I· want a prop for my declining years. (*She leans on the broom, which suddenly lets her down. She flings it aside.*) Wait till my boy Jack comes home from market—he's an example for you. He *never* chases the girls. Why, I've never seen him with a girl in my life !

(JACK *enters* L., *on " example". He is dressed in clothes that are far too small for him and has a small cap perched on the top of his head. With one hand he leads a large and magnificent goose by a string lightly fastened to its neck, with the other he leads* BETTY, *a beautiful young girl, who drags behind a little shyly.*)

JACK (*loudly and cheerfully*). Hullo, Mother ! Like my bird ?

(MOTHER GOOSE *spins round, not having seen them come in. She looks at them in awful silence for a moment or two.*)

MOTHER GOOSE (*meaningly*). Bird ? Which one ?

(PETER *and* JILL *laugh and nudge each other.*)

JACK (*carefully releasing the string from the* GOOSE'S *neck*). Why, this one, of course ! Beauty, isn't she ?

(*He stands back to admire the* GOOSE, *who walks with a slow and magnificent tread to* MOTHER GOOSE *and rubs its head affectionately against her skirt.* MOTHER GOOSE *pats and strokes it and makes clucking noises.*)

Guaranteed a good layer, and I got her in the market for *a mere song* !

MOTHER GOOSE. A mere song ? And what did you pay for the other one ? A grand opera ?

JACK. Don't be silly, Mother. I didn't pay anything for Betty. She kindly offered to come and work for us and look after the geese. *We've* got to pay *her* !

MOTHER GOOSE. Delighted ! (*Realizing.*) WHA-AT ! And how much ? A couple of choruses ?

BETTY (*crossing to* C., *and speaking in a low, thrilling voice*). I'll work for *love*, Mother Goose !

(*She turns and makes tremendous "eyes" at* JACK *who goes all "coy" and embarrassed.*)

MOTHER GOOSE. Love ? What *is* this ? An epidemic starting ? It's running through the house like measles !

JACK (*moving to* L. *of* BETTY). Oh, let her stay, Mother. We could do with some more help.

JILL. Yes, this new goose looks a bit of a toff—she'll want some looking after.

MOTHER GOOSE (*to* BETTY). Oh, all right. Stay and mind the geese then. What's another mouth to have nothing to feed with ?

JACK. What shall we call my goose ?

PETER. What about Gertie ?

(*The* GOOSE *indicates extreme distaste.*)

BETTY. Oh, no, no ! Only goats are called Gertie.

JILL. I think it ought to be something grand and majestic. How about Esmerelda ?

(*The* GOOSE *shakes her head.*)

MOTHER GOOSE. I've got it ! *Ermyntrude* !

(*The* GOOSE *shows great pleasure.*)

There you are—she likes it ! (*To the* GOOSE.) Well, Erm, we're poor, and you'll have to take *pot luck* . . .

(*The* GOOSE *shivers, and draws away.*)

Oh, dear ! " Pot luck "—that was tactless of me ! She's sensitive, you know ! I'll have her psycho-analysed. (*Taking the* GOOSE *upstage.*) Come into the kitchen, *dear* ——

(*The* GOOSE *tries to run away*.)

— I should say, the " parlour " ——

(*The* GOOSE *yields. They go up.*)

— excuse us . . .

(*She exits, with the* GOOSE, *into the cottage.*)

JILL (*going to* BETTY). I hope you'll be happy here, Betty.
PETER. Of course she will. Mother Goose isn't so bad. Her bark's worse than her bite.
JACK. You mean her squawk's worse than her peck.
BETTY. Thank you, I'm sure I shall love being here.

(*She looks sideways at* JACK, *who gazes at her adoringly.*)

JILL (*indicating* JACK *and* BETTY). I think we ought to be tactful.
PETER. Quite ! (*Raising his voice.*) We'd better be getting back to work ! Good-bye !

(JACK *and* BETTY *behave as if they had not heard.*)

JILL. Good-bye !

(*There is no response.*)

Well, we've been polite, anyway !

(*They exeunt* R. JACK *and* BETTY *are left at* L.C., *gazing at each other. Bus.*)

BETTY (*looking at him mischievously*). What did you say ?
JACK. N-nothing. It must have been one of the geese.
BETTY (*crossing* R. *and looking around appraisingly*). It's nice here, isn't it ?
JACK. Yes, we've got every modern inconvenience, including a mortgage.
BETTY (*moving close,* R. *of* JACK ; *speaking artlessly*). Oh, I've never seen a mortgage. Are they pretty ?
JACK. A mortgage ? Oh, very ! One of those nice little things you borrow money on to pay off someone else you've borrowed from.
BETTY (*admiringly*). How clever you are, Jack ! My great, big, strong, beautiful man ! (*She moves closer still.*)

JACK (*flexing his muscles proudly*). Well, I must **say** you're pretty observant ! (*Looking her up and down.*) You're a nice little thing, too. (*Hesitantly.*) Er—I say, Betty, how about us going out sometimes ? (*Bus. between each phrase.*) How about being my girl ? Couldn't we be engaged ? Let's get married !

BETTY. O-o-oh, Jack ! You are a quick worker ! This must be love at first sight ! (*Wriggling.*) O-o-oh — JACKY !

No. 3. DUET ..   .. (JACK *and* BETTY)

(*After the Number* JACK *puts his arm round* BETTY *and leads her to the seat,* R. *They sit and look at each other adoringly.* (*Music.*) SIR JASPER JABBERWOCK *with* BILL *and* BERT, *his bailiffs, enter* L. SIR JASPER *is the traditional wicked Squire. He has dark, curling moustaches and carries a hunting crop.* BILL *and* BERT *are just a pair of shabby ruffians.*)

SIR JASPER (*heartily*). Well, here we **are**—right at the seat of operations.

BILL (*laconically*). You're too late—it's occupied.

SIR JASPER. What is ?

BILL (*pointing to the seat where* JACK *and* BETTY *are now kissing each other*). The seat of operations.

SIR JASPER (*turning sharply and seeing* JACK). Ha-a-a-a ! So *this* is how that young jackanapes wastes his time instead of working to pay the rent ! (*Shouting to* JACK.) Hey, you !

(JACK *jumps up and pushes* BETTY *away hastily.*)

Where's Mother Goose ?

JACK (*pointing wildly to the cottage door*). In there ! Er—excuse me, I've got to see a hen about an egg.

He takes BETTY'S *hand and they dash off* R.   SIR JASPER *goes to the cottage door and knocks on it with his whip several times but there is no reply.*)

SIR JASPER. Ha-a-a ! She ignores muh ! She spurns muh ! Very well—(*Turning to* BILL *and* BERT.) Come, my beefy, battling bailiffs, we will burst . . . (*He draws a deep breath, puts his shoulder to the door and pushes hard.*)

BILL.   He will, too, if he goes on like this !
SIR JASPER (*after a pause for breath*).   Open the door ! Now, heave with me, my hearties !

(BERT *and* BILL *go up to the door.*)

BERT (*as they all push against the door*).   All this burstin' and 'eavin' don't suit my delicate constitution at all.   I'll need a stimulant after this.
SIR JASPER.   Stop !   We will change our tactics.
BILL.   I didn't bring any with me.
BERT.   Mine haven't come home from the laundry.
SIR JASPER.   We will rush our objective from here.

(*He retreats down* C. *and the bailiffs range themselves one each side.*)

Now, when I say go, we will make a concerted dash and hurl ourselves at the door and it should yield to our combined force.   Now—are we r-r-ready ?

(*All stand poised with right foot forward.*)

Steady—*go* !

(*They rush forward and throw themselves at the door just as* MOTHER GOOSE *opens it.   They all fall flat and she steps over them calmly and walks down* C.)

MOTHER GOOSE.   That's funny !   I could have sworn I heard a knock a moment ago.

(SIR JASPER *bellows unintelligibly as he tries to extricate himself from the other two, and* MOTHER GOOSE *turns and sees them.*)

No, don't get up !   I like the sensation of having three men at my feet.   I haven't even had one since I bought my last pair of shoes.   It makes me feel all girlish and oomph-ish !

(*By this time the three men are up and dusting themselves down.*)

Sir Jasper (*furiously*). Mother Goose, where is the rent ?

Mother Goose (*shocked*). How should I know ? Don't ask me where you've torn your clothes ! It serves you right for playing ring o' roses on my doorstep.

Sir Jasper. Don't trifle with me, woman ! You owe six months' rent ! If you can't pay we're going to eliminate you !

Mother Goose. Illuminate me ? Ah, well, I shan't be the first old ruin to be flood-lit !

Bert. We're going to kick you out, lady !

Mother Goose. How dare you call me a lady ? I won't have it ! And I won't have you kicking me out, lock, stock, and possibly barrel . . .

Sir Jasper (*roaring*). Then pay me my rent !

Mother Goose (*moving down* L.C. *with great dignity*). I will pay you in full when my cheque comes from my late husband's bankers.

Sir Jasper. I know *his* bank—the one where the wild thyme grows ! (*Turning to* Bill *and* Bert.) Get her sticks out, boys. We'll sell her up here and now.

Bill ⎫
Bert ⎭ (*together, as they dash into the cottage*). Yoicks ! Tally-ho !

(*They bring out an old three-legged chair, an enormous aspidistra, a moth-eaten fur, etc. They arrange them* c. *and* Sir Jasper *gets ready for an auction.* Peter *and* Jill *enter* R., *followed by the* Villagers *and* Milkmaids, *chattering excitedly.*)

Peter. What's happening here ?

Mother Goose. Oh, my priceless heirlooms ! Look at them ! Been in the Goose family ever since the first Gander landed in the soup.

Jill. What a shame, mother !

Sir Jasper. Roll up ! Roll up ! (*Holding up the disreputable fur.*) What offers for this beautiful and elegant fur, ladies and gentlemen ? (*He holds it at arm's length.*) Here you see a perfect example of a smelt—I mean, a pelt—that has only mellowed with the years. Its beauty has no rivals. (*Holding his nose.*) Put it in a room with a skunk and the skunk would walk out disheartened. What offers ?

A VOICE. Twopence ha'penny !

MOTHER GOOSE (*swiftly*). Twopence three farthings. Had you last !

SIR JASPER (*laughing with false jocularity*). Come, come now ! Have you no sense of values ?

A VOICE. No, but we've got a sense of smell !

(*Laughter and renewed chatter.*)

MOTHER GOOSE. You won't have that if *I* can get at you.

PETER. Sixpence !

SIR JASPER. A handsome offer, sir. Sixpence I am bid. Any advance ? No ? Going—going—*gone* !

(*He thumps his hunting crop on the floor each time narrowly missing the toes of* BILL *and* BERT, *who leaps out of his way.* BILL *hands the fur to* PETER *and quickly pockets the sixpence in exchange.*)

PETER (*handing the fur to* JILL). Here you are, darling. Give it back to Mother Goose from her future son-in-law.

JILL. Oh, Peter, thank you !

(*She crosses* L. *and hands it to* MOTHER GOOSE *who takes it and lovingly strokes it.*)

MOTHER GOOSE. My poor old Tibby !

BERT (*handing a three-legged chair to* SIR JASPER). 'Ere you are, Guv. Try the old Chippendale.

SIR JASPER (*holding it aloft*). Ha ! A genuine antique ! What am I bid for this remarkable piece ? Note the unique design (*pointing to the broken stump of a leg*). Obviously pre-Health Service period. Now, don't all shout at once—one at a time, please !

A VOICE (*shouting like a coster*). Firewood ! Wood-o !

OLD MAN. Reckon it'll come in for the old 'ooman. I'll swap a good sized turnip for it, mister.

(*There is general laughter and cheers.*)

MOTHER GOOSE (*furiously*). Turnip yourself, you old mangold wurzel! That's my *boo-dwar* stool. Gimme back my property !

(*She goes to rush at* SIR JASPER *but* BILL *and* BERT *hold her back. Suddenly the loud cackle of a* GOOSE *is heard off. Enter* BETTY *and* JACK R., *followed by* ERMYNTRUDE, *who looks very smug and satisfied.* BETTY *is carrying very carefully a large golden egg.*)

BETTY (*excitedly*). Look ! Look what Ermyntrude has just laid !

(MOTHER GOOSE *hurries across* R., *and takes the egg.* JILL *and* PETER *follow.*)

MOTHER GOOSE (*in a hushed voice*). It's gold—solid gold !

(*The* VILLAGERS *crowd round the family to look,* SIR JASPER, BILL, *and* BERT *move* L. *and watch conspiratorially.*)

JACK. Coo ! Fourteen carat by the look of it ! Isn't Ermyntrude clever ?

(*The* GOOSE *smirks modestly.*)

How *does* she do it ?
PETER (*to* JILL). You'll be rich now, and forget about me . . .
MOTHER GOOSE. And about time, too !
JILL. I will not !
SIR JASPER. Pah ! It's an old brass door-knocker ! Pish and tush !
MOTHER GOOSE (*advancing to him, followed by the others*). Pish, tush, and probably fiddle-de-dee to you ! It's gold, and I'm buying that old cottage for a pigsty—as for you, get out, d'you hear ? Get out—GET OUT !

(*She makes to throw the egg at him;* JACK *snatches it just in time. The* CROWD *boo* SIR JASPER, BILL *and* BERT *off* L. *Re-group, with* MOTHER GOOSE C., *with the* GOOSE.)

I'll give him brass door-knockers ! Gimme that egg !
I'll take care of it. Gold ! Fortune for the Goose Family,
and all the village to share !

(*Cheers.*)

No. 4.   ENSEMBLE : " AN EGG A DAY " ..(FULL COMPANY)

(*To the tune of "Autumn Song".*)

'Tis a wonderful goose that has come to stay
And a very original egg to lay,
Now we've turned out the brokers we'll pay the rent
There's plenty to follow when that is spent !
Oh, what a marvellous time there'll be
Poverty's over for you and me
Sun may be shining, but *bother* the hay—
When an egg a day's keeping the brokers away !
  (DANCE—*finishing with repeat of last two lines.*)

CURTAIN.

In front of TABS :—
No. 5.   SONG (*with* CHORUS)   ..   (MOTHER GOOSE)

SCENE 2

SCENE.—*The Farmyard of* MOTHER GOOSE'S *cottage.*
*Everything is old and ramshackle. An old chicken house
up* L. *Horse trough up* C. *Wood pile down* R. *One
or two logs or tree stumps.*

When the CURTAIN *rises,* JACK *is pottering about with
a battered bucket near the chicken house. He is followed
about by* ERMYNTRUDE, *the goose.*

No. 6.   SONG   ..   ..   (JACK)

During the Number, the GOOSE *squats at* L., *nodding
approvingly, and joining in the dance steps for the refrain.*
JACK *attends to the chicken house, his back to* R.   SIR
JASPER *enters up* R. *He looks around cautiously. The*
GOOSE *pecks* JACK *to attract his attention to* SIR JASPER.

JACK (*without turning*).   Morning, Squire.
SIR JASPER (*condescendingly*).   Good morning, my man.
You're working for a change, I can see.
JACK.   I'm working for the wages I *never* see.
SIR JASPER.   I can well believe it.   The place is dropping
to bits.   If I were to sue your mother for damages it would
run into thousands of pounds.
JACK.   You've had it !   She hasn't got a thousand pence.
SIR JASPER.   Then she's quite likely to be slung in the
cooler.
JACK.   Slung in the cooler ?
SIR JASPER.   Clapped in the calabooze.
JACK.   Anything to do with booze suits her !
SIR JASPER (*roaring*).   Incarcerated in quod !   Put in
prison !
JACK (*singing in a high, nasal tone*).   "Don't send my muvver
to prison, sir, it's the first crime what's she's done . . ."
SIR JASPER (*thunderously*).   Silence, half-wit ! (*Drawing*

13

JACK *to* R.). *You* only have the means to save her, if you will !

JACK. Me ? How ?

SIR JASPER. If you'll give me that goose in payment of the rent we'll say no more about it.

(ERMYNTRUDE *at once advances menacingly on the* SQUIRE, *her neck extended and hissing loudly.* JACK *goes to her and puts his arm round her, checking her progress. The* SQUIRE *backs* R.C., *alarmed.*)

JACK. Oh, no, I couldn't do that. Ermyntrude doesn't like the idea, you can see that. (*Patting and soothing the* GOOSE.) All right, Ermy old girl, nasty man shan't have her then.

SIR JASPER (*furiously*). I'll wring her neck . . . (*He is interrupted by the* GOOSE *hissing and straining to get at him.*)

JACK. Stop it, stop it, I tell you ! She can't stand that sort of talk. She's very sensitive !

SIR JASPER (*controlling himself with an effort*). Well, if I can't have her, give me that egg she laid yesterday. If you pay me one of those each week for rent, that'll do. Now, say you'll do that.

JACK. You'll do that.

SIR JASPER. No, no, you lunatic ! Promise me you'll give me an egg a week, and give me the first one now.

JACK. Oh, well ! If that's all you want, it'll be worth it ! (*He goes to the chicken house, produces the egg, and gives it to* SIR JASPER.) And no more about prison, *please !*

SIR JASPER. That remains to be seen ! Let there be an egg every Monday—or—broad arrows ! Ha ! HA !

(*He exits, laughing.* JACK *puts out his tongue, and then cuddles the* GOOSE, *who is annoyed.* PETER *enters* R.)

PETER. What's the meaning of this, Jack ? I've just passed the Squire with your goose's golden egg. Has he stolen it ?

JACK (*unconcernedly*). No, I gave it to him.

PETER (*staggered*). What ! ! *Gave* it to him ? Why ?

JACK. To pay the rent. I promised him one every Monday morning, too, so I hope Ermyntrude won't let us down. (*To the* GOOSE.) You won't, will you, darling ?

(*The* GOOSE *sniffs and tosses her head.*)

PETER. Jack ! You're hopeless ! Do you realize what you've done ?

JACK (*smugly*). Paid the rent and saved mother from prison.

PETER (*explosively*). Rubbish ! What you've done is to pay the rent for at least a year for this tumble-down old place. You've been swindled, Jack !

JACK. Oh, but he said he could make mother pay thousands of pounds in damages.

PETER. Damages for what ? *He's* the landlord, silly. *He* has to repair this place. Why, you could sue him.

JACK (*blankly*). Oh !

(ERMYNTRUDE *sidles up to him.*)

PETER. Oh, well, the damage is done now, only don't let him have any more, Jack.

JACK. I won't. I haven't got any more—yet.

(BETTY, SUSIE *and* SAM *enter* R., *followed by* VILLAGERS, *all carrying baskets.*)

JACK. Hullo, where are you off to ?

BETTY. We're going to market, Jack. Coming ?

JACK (*miserably*). No, I haven't got any money to spend.

SAM. Nonsense ! You've got that golden egg to sell.

JACK. W-w-w-well . . . (*Moving away.*) Oh, good gracious ! What *have* I done ?

SUSIE. Oh, come on, Jack. You can buy something nice for Betty.

(JACK *wails.*)

PETER. Oh, leave him alone. Come and help me, Jack, and tell me your troubles at the same time.

(*They exeunt,* L., *followed by* ERMYNTRUDE.)

No. 7. MARKETING SONG .. (BETTY, SUSIE, SAM *and*
CHORUS)

(To be sung to the tune of "The Maypole.")

BETTY.   Come my lads and lassies, away . . .
             For this is our market day,
             Customers require, if you please
             Milk and butter, eggs and cheese
SAM &   So to the market we will hie
SUSIE.   We have goods to sell and buy.
ALL.   So to the market we will hie
             We have goods to sell and buy.
BETTY.   Sweethearts, friends, await us there
             Round the market and the fair,
             Let us join the merry throng
             Fill the day with happy song.
SAM &   So to the market we will haste
SUSIE.   There the joy of life to taste.
ALL.   So to the market we will haste
             There the joy of life to taste.
BETTY.   Laces, satins or a pie,
             Toffee apples you may buy,
             Dainty ribbons for your hair,
             Jewels—perfumes, if you dare !
SAM &   So to the market let's away
SUSIE.   And enjoy it while we may.
ALL.   So to the market let's away,
             And enjoy it while we may !

(DANCE *to the music of the above.*)

(MOTHER GOOSE *enters* R., *carrying a large basket of eggs.
She is wearing the ancient fur and an old hat with a very
tall feather.*)

MOTHER GOOSE. Now then, now then, get a move on,
or the market will be over.

BETTY. All right, Mother Goose, we're just going.

MOTHER GOOSE. I'm coming on later with this, so tell
the customers what to expect. (*She bangs the basket down
with a crash.*)

SAM. Scrambled eggs ! O.K. !

(*He exits, with* SUSIE, BETTY, *and* CHORUS, *laughing and chattering.* MOTHER GOOSE *is left staring at the basket.*)

MOTHER GOOSE (*after a pause*). And d'you know—I believe he's right ! Yah ! (*She kicks the basket* R., *and calls.*) Jack ! Jack ! Where *is* that tiresome boy ?

(JACK *enters* L., *slowly. He is very nervous.*)

JACK.   H-here I am !
MOTHER GOOSE (*turning*). At last ! I'm just going to market with these paltry common hens' eggs, and I want that lovely big golden egg to sell as well. (*With the air of a duchess.*) Just hand it to meh, will yoh !

(JACK *gulps, grins in a sickly way, and fidgets.*)

JACK.   Golden egg ? (*Playing for time.*) What golden egg ?
MOTHER GOOSE (*raising her eyes*). *What* golden egg, he says, as if we've got the garden *paved* with them ! Did you *ever* ! (*Suddenly shouting.*) *The* golden egg, stoopid ! (*Dancing with rage.*) The golden egg the goose laid ! The golden egg the goose laid !
JACK (*very hurt*). All right, Mother, you needn't shout. I'm not deaf or daft.
MOTHER GOOSE. You're daft, all right. You always did take after your father's side of the family. Now, look sharp—get that egg !
JACK (*shifting uncomfortably*). Well, you see, Mother, I'll tell you . . .
MOTHER GOOSE (*sharply*). *What* are you trying to tell me ?
JACK (*speaking very quickly*). I'm trying to tell you that I told him I'd tell you what I told him.
MOTHER GOOSE (*looking a little dazed*). You're trying to tell *me* that you told *him* you'd tell *me* what you told *him* ?
JACK.   That's right, Mother.
MOTHER GOOSE (*ominously*). Who's " him " ?
JACK.   Well, I'm trying to tell you . . .
MOTHER GOOSE (*advancing on him menacingly*). Out with it—who's this mysterious " him " ?

JACK. The Squire, of course. That's what I was trying to tell you.

MOTHER GOOSE. And what smart business deal did you have with *him* ?

JACK. None at all. I just gave him the golden egg instead of the rent.

(*A pause,* MOTHER GOOSE *stares at* JACK.)

MOTHER GOOSE. *You what* ?

JACK. You heard. It saved you from going to prison, and a fat lot of thanks I get for it.

MOTHER GOOSE. Saved me from fiddlesticks ! Oh, the worm ! The snake-in-the-grass, the toad-in-the-hole ! To think he could have swindled an innocent boy like that. I'll get even with him yet, though. You wait !

(*A loud cackling noise is heard off and* JILL *enters* L., *staggering under the weight of an enormous golden egg. She is followed by* ERMYNTRUDE, *looking very proud.*)

JILL (*puffing excitedly*). Look ! Look ! *Another* golden egg and twice the size of the first one !

JACK (*going to* ERMYNTRUDE). Good old Ermyntrude ! You've just saved my bacon.

MOTHER GOOSE. Bacon ? That's not going with bacon —that's going to make us rich—the richest family in Ptomania. Hooray ! (*She does a few dance steps and falls.*)

JILL. Oh, Mother ! What are we going to do now ?

MOTHER GOOSE. I'll go straight to the estate agents and see what baronial castles they have on their books, and not any of your pre-fabs, either !

No. 7a. REPRISE REFRAIN . . ."AN EGG A DAY" .. ..
(MOTHER GOOSE, JACK *and* JILL)

CURTAIN.

ACT I. INTERLUDE.

In Front of TABS *during Scene Change.*

Soft music. ERMYNTRUDE *enters* L. *and walks slowly to* C.
Enter FAIRY SUNBEAM R. *She approaches* ERMYNTRUDE
gently.

FAIRY. Dear Princess Ermyntrude, you've been
Most kind to Mother Goose, I've seen
The golden eggs you've given her
To save her family from despair.
(GOOSE *struts about proudly.*)
But if the love of gold should prove
To take from Mother Goose her love
Of simple things, and give instead
That curse of mortals, swollen-head,
Then back to Goose Land you must fly
And she return to poverty.

*(There is a sudden darkening of the scene, two flashes of
lightning and a rumble of thunder. The music changes to a
more tempestuous character. When the* LIGHTS *go up again
dimly, the* DEMON KING *is standing* L.C.)

DEMON (*very dramatically*).
I am the Spirit of Vanity and Greed,
My power shall thwart the Princess's good
deed,
For Mother Goose shall feel temptation's
power
And lose her new-found riches in that hour !
FAIRY Begone, foul Demon, with your evil threat !
I'll see that Mother Goose shall triumph yet !
DEMON (*with a sinister cackle*).
The fight is on, O Queen, 'twixt you and me,
And who shall be the victor ?

(*There is a burst of fiendish laughter as the stage darkens again.*)

We shall see !

(*He disappears in a black-out. As the lights rise again* ERMYNTRUDE *is seen with her head bent in a downcast attitude.*)

FAIRY (*sweetly*). Take heart, dear Golden Goose, whate'er befall
I shall be with you, well within your call.

No. 8. SONG   ..   ..   ..   FAIRY SUNBEAM

(*She exits* R. *For a moment* ERMYNTRUDE *is left alone, then raises her head proudly and walks off* R. *with stately, measured tread.*)

CURTAIN.

SCENE 3.

SCENE.—*A clearing in the forest.*

A sloping bank up C. *Sky beyond. The light is dim among the trees at the back. There is a large log at* L. *At the back, up* R., *is a large stone with a flat surface.*

On the rise of the CURTAIN, *the stage is empty. (Suggested music—"The Teddy Bear's Picnic," with weird variations.)* BILL *and* BERT *slowly emerge from behind the tree up* L., *and advance with exaggerated caution down* C., *saying "Sh-h-h !" and looking round fearfully as they go. An owl hoots and they leap in terror and rush back to the cover of the trees, a moment later repeating bus. of advancing cautiously on tip-toe down* C. *They are standing side by side in a listening attitude, clearly terrified, when* SIR JASPER *enters from up* C. *He advances stealthily on* BILL *and* BERT *and suddenly claps a hand on each of their shoulders. They scream and gibber incoherently, too frightened to look up and see who holds them.*

BILL (*finding his voice at last*). All right, h'orficer, I'll come quietly.

BERT. I swear I never done it, sergeant ! I can prove me innocence !

BILL (*trembling*). S'right ! Pure as the driven snow at Christmas time. We're the Babes in the Wood !

SIR JASPER (*softly*). Well, I'm Santa Claus. (*Suddenly shouting.*) And I'm going to knock your blocks off !

(BILL *and* BERT *look up to see who holds them.*)

BILL Oh, my great-aunt Miranda !

BERT. 'Tisn't—it's the old—it's the old . . . (*He stops short as he sees* SIR JASPER'S *steely eye.*) It's 'im !

SIR JASPER. Yes—'im—ME ! (*Menacingly.*) What are you two playing at ? Babes in the Wood ! Well, there won't be anything left for the birds to cover with leaves

21

by the time *I've* done with you if you don't pay attention
to *me* ! (*He pushes them away forcefully and they reel and
stagger round the stage*, R. *and* L., *singing* " Here we go round
the mulberry bush ".)

SIR JASPER (*roaring*). Stop ! This is too much !

BILL (*still dancing*). We'll cut some of it if you like then.

SIR JASPER. Come here, you gibbering, jumping jackanapes !

BERT. Do you think he meant us ?

SIR JASPER. Now, listen, lunatics. I want to hatch out
a plot.

(BILL *makes a terrific clucking noise.*)

What *are* you doing ?

BILL. Hatching out a plot. That's what you want,
isn't it ?

SIR JASPER. You can cluck *after* you've produced the
egg—not before, but—(*with meaning*)—the egg's got to be
a *golden* one.

BERT. A golden egg ? You mean—like . . . ?

SIR JASPER. Yes ! I mean like Mother Goose's goose
lays.

BILL. But she's the only one who's got the recipe. I've
looked all through Mrs Beeton and can't find it.

BERT (*in a grumbling tone*). Well, after all, Guv'nor,
you can't expect us to lay *eggs*. You didn't engage us for
that. I'll lay two to one on the 2.30 ; I'll lay a foundation
stone if you like, but eggs—no ! My Union wouldn't let
me.

BILL. They'd call you a blackleg-horn if you did.

(BERT *groans at the pun.*)

SIR JASPER (*in exasperation*). If you two don't stop being
funny there won't be any wages for you this week.

BERT. That won't make no difference.

BILL. There haven't been any for the past fifty-two
weeks.

SIR JASPER. Well, you can have them in full when you
get hold of the golden goose for me.

BERT. You mean—swipe her ? Pinch, or purloin her ?

SIR JASPER. Don't be vulgar ! I mean snitch her—*and* kill her.

BILL (*covering his face with his hands*). Oh, no, not that ! We couldn't wring her little white necky-wecky !

BERT (*to* SIR JASPER). Why don't you do your own dirty work ?

SIR JASPER (*childishly*). Because she hisses at me and I'm afraid she'll peck me. (*Musing.*) She must be full of those golden eggs. Why wait for a miserable one a day ? (*To* BILL *and* BERT.) If you kill her, *I* shall have them all. I shall be a wealthy man.

BERT (*to* BILL). Hear that, Bill ? If *we* kill her, *he'll* be a wealthy man ! (*Laughs bitterly.*)

BILL. I couldn't bring myself to kill her if she was stuffed with diamonds.

SIR JASPER. She'll be stuffed with sage and onions when I've finished with her.

BILL (*showing a sudden interest*). Will you have apple sauce and thick gravy with her ?

SIR JASPER. We'll have *all* the trimmings—and wash her down with *champagne*.

BILL. Well, that's different. Such a change from Dettol !

BERT. I'll do it on a 10 per cent. commission basis.

SIR JASPER (*threateningly*). You'll do it because *I* say so, you piffling pair of poachers ! Now listen—Mother Goose is going to give a housewarming . . .

BILL (*clasping his hands*). Oh, *do* say we've been invitahd! I LERVE a parteh ! (*Bus.*)

(BERT *copies him.*)

SIR JASPER (*ignoring them*). Now, while I am charming all the company with my sparkling conversation, my ready wit and what-not——

(BILL *and* BERT *look at each other and groan.*)

—you will find an opportunity to entice the golden goose away to the forest. You will bring her here and I will meet you—*at midnight*.

BERT. What night ?

SIR JASPER (*shouting*). Midnight !

(BILL *and* BERT *shiver in mock fear*.)

BILL. O-o-oh ! Couldn't you make it a little earlier—say just after we've had our 'levenses in the morning ?

SIR JASPER (*menacingly*). I said *midnight* and midnight it shall be !

BERT. That'll mean double time and special rates for night shift.

SIR JASPER. No matter ! It must be done !

No. 9.   TRIO : " THREE BOUNCING BUCCANEERS "
                              (SIR JASPER, BILL *and* BERT)

(*To be sung to the tune of "A-hunting We Will Go".*)

ALL.	We are three bouncing buccaneers,
	We care not what we do !
SIR JASPER.	We're fearless, brave and fairly strong,
BILL *and* BERT.	We're fearless, brave and fairly strong,
SIR JASPER.	We're dark and tall and handsome too,
BILL *and* BERT.	We're tall and handsome too !
ALL.	The rage of all the girls !
	The rage of all the girls !
	The ra-age of a-all the gur-hur-hur-
	hurls !
	When a-courting we do go !
	Tan-tivy, tan-tivy, tan-tivy !
	A-courting we will go !
ALL.	We are three robbers full of zeal
	We care not who we rob.
SIR JASPER.	We thieve and plunder, pick and steal
BILL *and* BERT.	We only ask a simple meal
SIR JASPER.	It's just a normal daily job !
BILL *and* BERT.	A normal daily job !
ALL.	We're going to steal an egg !
	We're going to steal an egg !
	Oh, rather than beg, we'd swipe an egg,
	So a-stealing we will go.

ALL	We are three jolly murderers Our 'earts are 'orribly 'ard !
SIR JASPER.	Established now for years and years
BILL *and* BERT.	For years and years and years and years
SIR JASPER.	As stated on our business card
BILL *and* BERT.	As stated on our card !
ALL.	We mean to cook our goose And then go on the loose ! Inviting—exciting—to nobble a goose ! So a-slaughtering we will go !
CHORUS *and* DANCE.	A-slaughtering we will go ! A-slaughtering we will go ! So gory a story will end in a noose But a-slaughtering we must go !

(*A* BURLESQUE *of a* DAINTY DANCE *is done to this.* CHORUS
enter and join in for FINALE *of* ACT.)

CURTAIN.

ACT II.

SCENE I.

SCENE.—*The interior of* MOTHER GOOSE'S *Castle.*

A wide arch up C., *leading by broad steps to a rostrum.* *Arched entrances* R. *and* L. *The scene to be as ornate as possible, with divans and a few chairs as required.*

When the CURTAIN *rises, the* CHORUS *of* GUESTS *(including* SAM *and* SUSIE) *are on the stage, singing—and dancing.*

No. 10.   OPENING CHORUS   ..   (THE COMPANY)

During the dance following the CHORUS, *which should be a waltz,* SAM *and* SUSIE *dance together.* *The music should now be very soft as they dance across* C.

SAM.   Where's Mother Goose ?
SUSIE.   Oh, she's still titivating.

(They dance across. *The music continues very softly.* *A* FLUNKEY *appears on the rostrum* C.)

FLUNKEY (*in stentorian tones*).   Sir Jasper Jabberwock !

*(*SIR JASPER *appears.* *The* CHORUS, *grouped* R. *and* L., "boo" *loudly, and go on chattering to each other, swaying or dancing to the music.* SIR JASPER *comes down, and goes* R. *and takes a glass of wine from a* FLUNKEY *there as* BERT *and* BILL *appear up* C.)

and his battling bailiffs, Mr Bert Bashem and Mr Bill Biffem !

(Cat-calls. *The crowd ignore them as they come down, trip on the bottom step and cross to* SIR JASPER. *They are about to take glasses of wine when the* FLUNKEY *turns and exits.* *Bus.*)

Her Grease the Goose !

(*Cheers.* ERMYNTRUDE *appears up* C., *comes down, and shakes
hands with guests from* R. *to* L., *and exits* L. *The chattering
and soft music continues.*)

SIR JASPER (*conspiratorially*).   Now's your chance—
follow her—grab her—take her off by the back door !
BERT. Don't rush me ! Don't rush me ! What about
supper ?
SIR JASPER. Do as I say !
BILL. I can't pinch a goose on an empty stummick !
FLUNKEY (*up* C.). Mother Goose and her little Goslings !
SIR JASPER.   Too late !

(MOTHER GOOSE *has appeared, followed by* JACK, JILL *and
then* BETTY. MOTHER GOOSE *is dressed in a most fantastic
and extravagant costume with a huge wobbly tiara. They
descend. The children and* BETTY *move to* L.C.)

MOTHER GOOSE (*at* C.; *in very refined tones*). Good
evening—good evening—good evening, everybodeh ! How-
de-do, Sir Jaspah ! Soo delayted to see yoh, old cock !
(*Bus. with dress, tiara, etc.*)
SIR JASPER. Charmed ! And what a magnificent en-
semble you're wearing !
MOTHER GOOSE. You don't mean to tell me it's showing ?
(*Bus.*) As for this tirara ! The skewers I've bent fixing it
you wouldn't berlieve !
SUSIE.   Never mind, you look lovely !
GUESTS (*shouting*).   Good old Mother Goose !
MOTHER GOOSE. Thank you . . . eh ? Good *what*
Mother Goose ?
GUESTS. Good *gracious* Mother Goose !
MOTHER GOOSE. That's better. And let me tell you,
I'm Lady Goose-Gog now, with one of those little hori-
zontal bars between the Goose and the Gog.
SAM. And don't the children look just grand !

(JACK *and* BETTY *look very embarrassed and glum.* JILL *is
standing with them, even more unhappy because* PETER *is
absent.* MOTHER GOOSE *looks at them with disgust.*)

MOTHER GOOSE.   I ask you !

(*She looks them up and down. They gaze at the ground, and shuffle.*)

(*In a hushed voice.*) The *wreaths* have just arrived. (*To the audience, wiping her eyes.*) The cortège will move off in a few moments. (*To the others, savagely.*) Cheer up, can't yer ? (*To the audience.*) Very well, then, I'll *sing* ! And don't blame me—you've brought it on yourselves !

No. 11. SONG   ..   (MOTHER GOOSE *and* CHORUS)

(*This may be followed by a dance to refrain.*)

JACK (*to* MOTHER GOOSE). Mum, can't we have supper now ?

MOTHER GOOSE. Oh, is *that* what it is ? I don't know where you put it ! (*To* SIR JASPER.) The chips that boy packs away . . . (*Shouting towards* R.) Is that corned beef and pickles ready ?

(*The* FLUNKEY *appears* R.)

FLUNKEY. Suppah is sahved !

MOTHER GOOSE. And about time, too ! Come and get it !

(*The* GUESTS *move to exits* R., *and go off in pairs.* BERT *and* BILL *go stealthily up* C. *and across* L., *as* SIR JASPER *engages* MOTHER GOOSE. JACK, JILL, *and* BETTY *confer at* L. BERT *and* BILL *exit up* L., *quietly.*)

SIR JASPER. Will you honour me with your company at the festive board, dear Lady Goose-Gog ?

MOTHER GOOSE. We'll have the run of our teeth together, yes !

JACK (*moving to behind* MOTHER GOOSE *and tugging at her dress*). Mum !

MOTHER GOOSE. Leggo ! (*To* SIR JASPER.) Do yew *know* . . .

JACK (*same bus.*). Mum—I want to speak to you !

MOTHER GOOSE (*turning and looking him up and down*). Would you ber*lieve* it ?

JACK. I wanted to ask you if . . .

MOTHER GOOSE (*in an undertone*). Can't you see I'm just hypnotising the Squire—at least, I think I am—I've got him just where I want him . . .

SIR JASPER (*bawling furiously*). Are you or are you not coming in to supper, you old hag ?

MOTHER GOOSE (*giving a violent start*). Or am I wrong ? (*Turning on* SIR JASPER.) Go by yourself, you moth-eaten bag of misery, and may it choke you !

SIR JASPER.   T'chah !

(*He flings off*, R.)

MOTHER GOOSE (*calling after him*). And mind the step !

(*Crash off* R.)

Too late—splendid ! (*To* JACK.) There you are—you've spoiled your sister's chances ! I'd set my heart on her being Lady Jasper Jabberwock.

JILL. I never would ! I mean to marry Peter ! I think you're cruel not to invite him.

MOTHER GOOSE. What ! A ploughman—and us with all this boodle, and a castle to live in !

JACK. We don't want a castle—Jill wants Peter, and I want Betty ! We want to be engaged.

BETTY. We want to be husband and wife.

JACK. I want to be the husband, and Betty the wife.

MOTHER GOOSE. How very original ! Well, you can't ! It's nonsense !

JACK.   It's love.

MOTHER GOOSE. What's the difference ? You—heir to the Goose-Gog millions, marrying a milkmaid ! Ha !

BETTY. I'm a *goose-girl*—and I wouldn't be that, if I married Jack !

MOTHER GOOSE (*loftily*). May that as it be—I mean— bay me as it thee . . .

JACK.   You mean, be may as it that.

JILL.   She means be mat as it they.

MOTHER GOOSE (*shouting*). Be thee as it me ! Now I'm in a muddle—anyway, I have higher ambitions for my children than ploughmen or goose-girls.

JACK. If you don't say 'yes' I'm going to leave home.

JILL. And I shall marry Peter—you can marry Sir Jasper yourself !

MOTHER GOOSE. And I will too, if I have half a chance—I mean if I have any more nonsense.

BETTY. All you think about is your wretched ambitions.

JACK. Money—money—money.

JILL. You don't care how miserable we are ! Just because you're old and ugly yourself.

MOTHER GOOSE. *What !*

JILL. You're jealous of me and Peter and Jack and Betty—oh, yes, you are.

MOTHER GOOSE. Ooh, how cruel.

(PETER *enters* L., *with* ERMYNTRUDE.)

PETER. Excuse me interrupting the jollification, but do you want this goose, or don't you ?

MOTHER GOOSE. Of course I want her ! How dare you tamper with her ?

PETER. I'm not tampering—I'm returning her to you. I've just saved her from those burgling bailiffs, Bert and Bill !

MOTHER GOOSE. What ! (*She takes* ERMYNTRUDE *up* C., *and puts her arms round her.*)

JILL. Oh, Peter ! How splendid of you ! Come along and have some supper. (*She drags him towards* R.)

MOTHER GOOSE. No !

(JILL *and* PETER *exit* R.)

JACK. Haven't you any gratitude ? Jill is right—you've been spoilt by this money—you're not a bit like the Mother Goose we used to have ! You're all mean, and spiteful, and stuck up and . . .

MOTHER GOOSE. And old—and ugly—I know ! I know ! Go away and leave me to my misery !

JACK. To your conscience !

(*He runs off* R. *with* BETTY.)

MOTHER GOOSE. Conscience ? I never heard of such a thing !

(ERMYNTRUDE *quacks.*)

(*Sitting.*) Yes—you understand, don't you Ermyntrude ? Old ! Ugly ! Stuck up ! Jealous ! That's what my children think of me after I've slaved fingers to the bone, kept my shoulder to the wheel, my hand to the plough and my nose to the grindstone—yes, look at it *now* ! And as soon as I get a bit of money and give them a good home and all the discomforts of modern luxury—they don't appreciate it ! It's cruel ! I wish I knew of some charm to make me young and beautiful as well as rich ! That'd shake 'em !

(ERMYNTRUDE *quacks three times.*)

(BLACK OUT. MOTHER GOOSE *screams. The lights go on—a green spot—revealing the* DEMON KING *up* C. MOTHER GOOSE *and* ERMYNTRUDE *are standing* R.C.)

Lumme ! Who's this ? I never invited you !

DEMON KING (*suavely*).
　　　　I heard the quack, the wish, and came
　　　　To give you all the things you name—
　　　　Youth—beauty—riches—all you will,
　　　　If one condition you fulfil.
MOTHER GOOSE. Well, if it's one of these forms to fill up . . .
DEMON KING (*interrupting with a gesture*).
　　　　Go to the forest, all alone,
　　　　At midnight—on the Wishing Stone
　　　　Repeat the magic incantation
　　　　And then—behold the transformation !
MOTHER GOOSE. What ? Alone—at midnight ? An innocent little thing like me ?
DEMON KING.
　　　　Not quite alone, for you must take
　　　　The Golden Goose, and she will make
　　　　Your wish come true, so don't forget——

(*He laughs, as the scene darkens.*)

——you'll be a youthful beauty yet !

(*A flash of lightning.* B.O. *The lights go up again. The* DEMON KING *has gone, and* FAIRY SUNBEAM *stands in his place. Soft music.*)

FAIRY SUNBEAM (*sorrowfully*).
    Oh, Mother Goose, you must not heed
    The Spirit of Vanity and Greed.
    His words are false—his promise vain—
    He cannot give you youth again !
MOTHER GOOSE. Oh, dear, I'm all of a doodah now. Anyway . . .
FAIRY SUNBEAM (*interrupting*).
    You must not go—'tis but a ruse
    For wicked men to steal the Goose
    So listen carefully to my warning
    Or—lose your riches by the morning !

(*The lights fade a little. The* FAIRY *exits* C. *The music ceases and the light brightens.*)

MOTHER GOOSE. Well, I can't be having *D.T.s* so early in the evening. No ! I'll take a chance ! The forest at midnight ! You and me !

(ERMYNTRUDE *shivers.*)

They're coming back from supper.

(*Voices and laughter off* R. *The music of the Waltz Song, No.* 10, *strikes up as the* GUESTS *begin to dance on.*)

Come on !

(*The principals and chorus now all dance on.* MOTHER GOOSE *seizes* SIR JASPER. *They dance as the entire company sings.*)

No. 12.   WALTZ SONG   ..   (FULL COMPANY)

TABS *close.*

INTERLUDE.

In front of TABS *during scene change—*

No. 13.   COMEDY DUET   ..   ..   BILL *and* BERT

SCENE 2.

SCENE.—*The Forest, as in Act I, Scene 3.   Night.*

When the CURTAIN rises the forest is bathed in a ghostly green light.   The DEMON KING is squatting on the wishing stone.   DEMON SPIRITS, dressed to represent Greed, Vanity, etc., etc., are dancing.

No. 14.   DEMON BALLET   ..   ..   ..   (DEMONS)

As the Ballet ends, there is a brilliant flash of lightning, and B.O.   Then soft moonlight fades in revealing an empty stage, the DEMONS and KING having vanished.   The wind moans and howls.   MOTHER GOOSE, wearing a cloak, and leading ERMYNTRUDE, enters up C.   The GOOSE is holding back.

MOTHER GOOSE (*wheedling, in a whining voice*).   Oh come on, Ermyn*trude* !   There's a good girl—I know it's past your bedtime but it's all in the cause of Youth and Beauty.   There's nothing to be afraid of——

(*An awful shriek of wind.*)

—noth-thuth-thuthing at all.   A-AH !   (*She shrieks.*) Practically !   (*She turns down* L.C.)

(ERMYNTRUDE *quacks loudly.* MOTHER GOOSE *screams and wheels round.*)

Don't *do* that !   Last time you quacked that gentleman in green turned up—which reminds me, there's the Wishing Stone !   But it hasn't struck twelve yet.

(*A howl of wind.   She turns* L. *to find a* GHOST *close to her. It has been lowered from above.*)

OW !   Good evening !   (*She is about to shake hands when the* GHOST *is raised out of sight.*)   Sorry you couldn't stop . . .

(*She turns* R. *to find another* GHOST *lowered close to her on the other side.*)

Oh—you got back all right ? How d'you . . .

(*The second* GHOST *is raised.* B.O. *Lightning. Lights up.*)

Oh, Mother ! I wish I hadn't come . . .

　　　(ERMYNTRUDE *quacks, and comes down.*)

Don't DO that ! Come and sit down.

(*They move to the log* L., *are about to sit, when the log is raised above* MOTHER GOOSE'S *head.*)

Going up! Haberdashery—groceries—kitchen utensils——

(*She sits on the ground. The log is lowered and rests on her lap.*)

—ground floor—carpets—bargain basement . . . Go *away*!

(*She pushes the log away, rises, seizes it, places it on the ground, and sits.* ERMYNTRUDE *perches on it. The wind howls.* GHOSTS *flit in and out. Lightning. Thunder.*)

Ermyntrude—l-l-listen t-t-to me ! And stop your t-t-teeth cha-cha-chattatattering ! Those aren't g-ghosts—it's only someone left their smalls on the line . . . Listen !

(SIR JASPER *and* BILL *and* BERT *heard off* R. *singing* "*We won't go home till morning.*")

Those dirty dogs again ! W-w-well, I never thought I'd be glad to see *that* gang of toughs. Let's hide, and hear no good of ourselves.

(*They hide behind a tree* L., *as* SIR JASPER *appears up* C. BILL *and* BERT *follow. He signals them to be silent, pointing* L.)

SIR JASPER. *Aha !*
BILL *and* BERT. Ha-*ha* !
SIR JASPER (*in a hoarse whisper*). Shut up ! She's behind that tree ! (*Loudly.*) This is the way that dear innocent helpless lady came, with that lovely tender unprotected bird ! Would that I might woo her !

BERT.   The bird ?
SIR JASPER.   No, fool ! The lady ! She fascinates me !
Her sweet innocence and fair ways, despite her age and
looks which might be worse but not much — she enthrals
me ! I long only to protect her in this dismal place. Is it
not so ?
BILL *and* BERT.   No—YES !
SIR JASPER.   Do you wish her any harm ?
BERT *and* BILL.   Yes—NO !
SIR JASPER.   Of course not ! But we must find her
whereabouts !
BERT *and* BILL.   And put 'em through the mangle !
SIR JASPER.   SHUT UP !
MOTHER GOOSE (*appearing* L. *with* ERMYNTRUDE). They—
I mean we—are here !
SIR JASPER.   Ah, dear lady—are you safe and sound ?

(BLACK OUT. *Then a period of flickering light in which the
characters and several ghosts are seen rushing about trying
to find each other, to cries of* " Where are you ? " "Can't
find you," " Ooh, I touched one ! " *etc., etc., and calling
to each other by name. Then the lights go up, and only
the four characters are there, with* ERMYNTRUDE.)

MOTHER GOOSE.   I love these Dodg'ems ! Have you
got another sixpence ? I must go on again !
SIR JASPER.   Come home with me, my little goose-gog !
MOTHER GOOSE. Never ! At least, not until I've got
what I came for !
SIR JASPER.   Shall we rest awhile ?
MOTHER GOOSE. Ooh, I'd *lerve* to ! Let me sew you to
your sheet !

(*She leads him* L. *The log rises and goes out of sight.*)

Standing room only in the one and ninepennies !

(*Shriek of wind.*)

BILL *and* BERT.   OW !
SIR JASPER.   Cowards all !
BERT.   Well, I know where I'd rather be !
BILL.   Same 'ere !
MOTHER GOOSE.   Me too !

SIR JASPER.   Quite so !

No. 15.   QUARTETTE. " I'D RATHER BE . . ."
        (MOTHER GOOSE, SIR JASPER, BILL *and* BERT)
        (AIR : " *Down among the Dead Men.*")

BERT.   There's an 'orrible feeling just round 'ere.
BILL.   Of goblins lurkin' rather near !
SIR JASPER.   I'm not afraid of demons dark,
MOTHER GOOSE.   For we're quite used to . . . (*local*)
Park !
ALL.   But all the same we'd rather be—
        *Down at Mother Reilly's
        Down at Mother Reilly's
        Down—down—down—down—
        Down at Mother Reilly's with a nice cupper tea !
                (*Dance steps.*)

BERT.   I 'eard an 'owl, and I 'eard a groan,
BILL.   And a devil came out all skin and bone !
SIR JASPER.   And a grizzly ghost in a winding sheet
MOTHER GOOSE.   Like the washing hung out in . .
(*local*) Street !
ALL.   We'd rather be, instead of here—
        Down at Mother Reilly's
        Down at Mother Reilly's
        Down—down—down—down—
        Down at Mother Reilly's with a bottle of beer !
                (*Dance steps.*)

BERT.   Oh, the place just reeks of gallows and chains,
BILL.   Of dangling bones and rusty stains,
SIR JASPER.   We do not grouse, of course, at that
MOTHER GOOSE.   After living at . . . (*local*) in a Council
flat !
ALL.   But on the whole we'd rather come
        Down to Mother Reilly's
        Down to Mother Reilly's
        Down—down—down—down—
        Down at Mother Reilly's, with a barrel of rum !

*NOTE : *Instead of " Mother Reilly's" a local public house, club, or
other place may be inserted.*

(DANCE . . . *during which* BERT *and* BILL *make off with* ERMYNTRUDE R., *unnoticed by* MOTHER GOOSE.)

(MOTHER GOOSE *is now at* C., *with* SIR JASPER *on her* R.)

SIR JASPER. Ah, that's better !
MOTHER GOOSE. D'you know, I believe we've driven all those demons away !
SIR JASPER. Having heard you sing, I am not surprised.
MOTHER GOOSE. You think you're very funny, don't you ? Well, let me tell you there's a lot of funnier things happening round here to-night, demons or no demons . . .

(BLACK OUT. *In flashes of light* DEMONS *and* GHOSTS *rush on.* SIR JASPER *and* MOTHER GOOSE *run around trying to dodge them, as before, colliding with them and each other.*)
During this :

MOTHER GOOSE. Help ! Help ! Mother ! Fire ! Murder ! (*ad. lib.*)
SIR JASPER. Fetch the police ! Nine-nine-nine ! Scotland Yard ! Fetch the Women's Institute ! (*ad. lib.*)

(LIGHTS *up.* SIR JASPER *is clutching* MOTHER GOOSE, *who shrieks, and pushes him away. He falls.*)

MOTHER GOOSE. Oh, Jassy—have they gone ? (*Looking around.*) Where are you ?
SIR JASPER (*on the ground*). Here !
MOTHER GOOSE. Then come upstairs at once—I'm frightened.
(SIR JASPER *rises.*)

Hiding in the basement—I never did !

(*Church clock booms the hour.*)

Midnight ! I've forgotten what I came for . . .
SIR JASPER. The washing . . .

MOTHER GOOSE. That's it—the washing . . . What d'you mean, " the washing " ? I've got it !
SIR JASPER.   The washing ?
MOTHER GOOSE. No—Wishing ! The Wishing Stone ! I'm going to try it out !
SIR JASPER. What are you talking about ?
MOTHER GOOSE. Never you mind. You're not to listen ! Go on ! Over there and put your hands over your eyes and your fingers in your ears—*if* you can reach them. Go on ! By the log !
SIR JASPER (*looking* L.). There isn't a log. (*He turns to* MOTHER GOOSE.)
MOTHER GOOSE.   Oh yes, there is !

(*The log is lowered to elbow height behind* SIR JASPER. *He turns, and leans his elbow on it as if it was a bar counter, throws a coin on it and calls :* Half a pint ! *A* DEMON *appears* L. *of the log, puts his face against* SIR JASPER'S *and gives a shriek of laughter.* SIR JASPER *faints over the log. In the meantime,* MOTHER GOOSE *has settled on the Wishing Stone up* R.C.)

Now then—wait for it ! Wait for it ! " Speak aloud the incantation—and then await the transformation " ! This is it ! (*She chants.*) I want to be young—oo-er !—and beautiful—lummy !—and rich—yippee ! I want to be young and beautiful and rich I want to be young and beautiful and rich I want to be . . . (*She pauses.*) Oooh ! I feel different already ! D'you know, I believe I've gone all young—or is it a spider down me back ? I'm sure I'm beautiful (*To* AUDIENCE.) Aren't I beautiful ? Yes, I said I was ! (*Or, " Ooh, you fibbers, I* am *! "*) Now let's try it on the dog ! (*She gets off the Stone and moves to* C.) You can look round now ! (*Coyly.*) Jass-sy ! Wakey-wakey ! You can look round now ! (*Savagely.*) Look round, you old dustbin !

(SIR JASPER *straightens up, and turns.*)

Oh, Jassy, I'm ever so young and beautiful and rich !
SIR JASPER.   Did you say rich !

MOTHER GOOSE. Oh, as rich as Creosote ! And very young !

SIR JASPER. Never mind trifles—you're *rich* ?

MOTHER GOOSE. Yes, and ever so beeyutiful !

SIR JASPER. Don't confuse the issue with unnecessary details ! You're rich—you have plenty of gold ?

MOTHER GOOSE. Gold ! Pooh ! Tush ! Why, in my garden the very rockeries are solid gold ! Oh, Jassy ! (*She goes to clasp him.*)

SIR JASPER. Splendid ! I'm off to get a special licence !

MOTHER GOOSE. Whaffor ?

SIR JASPER. To pull down the rockeries ! (*He rushes off* L.)

MOTHER GOOSE (*shouting after him*). Oy ! Ooh, you are unkind to meee ! Gertcha ! (*To the* AUDIENCE.) Aren't men *awful* ! Really, you never know what they're going to say next ! The other evening . . .

(PETER *enters up* C., *from* L. MOTHER GOOSE *sees him.*)

(*To the* AUDIENCE.) Oh, here's another ! Now I'm going to prove—*prove*, mark you, that the charm has worked !

(*She moves to* PETER *who has come down.*)

(*To* PETER.) Oh, good evernin' ! (*She sidles up, gives him a ' come-hither ' look, etc.*)

PETER (*not recognising her*). Oh, excuse me, madam, but has an ugly old woman come this way ?

MOTHER GOOSE (*to the* AUDIENCE). It's worked ! (*To* PETER.) Not since I came !

PETER. I'm looking for Mother Goose. She's gone off by herself, the silly old geezer . . .

MOTHER GOOSE (*forgetting*). 'Oo are you calling a silly old geezer ?

PETER. Old Mother Goose.

MOTHER GOOSE. Oh, that's different ! (*Digging him in the ribs.*) P'raps she's not so old as you think . . . (*Bus.*)

PETER. Hey ! None of that ! There's only one girl in the world for me, but unfortunately it happens to be this stupid old hay-bag's daughter——

(MOTHER GOOSE *reacts*.)

—but I mean to marry her whatever the wretched old crone has to say . . .

(JACK *enters* L. *He recognises* MOTHER GOOSE.)

JACK (*excitedly*). Oh, there you are, Mother !
MOTHER GOOSE (*wheeling round*). EH ! Jack ! He knows me !
PETER (*retreating in astonishment*). Mother Goose !
JACK. We've searched everywhere for you ! What on earth made you come to the forest all alone ?
MOTHER GOOSE. You mean to say you still recognise me ?
JACK. Of course I do ! Why shouldn't I ?
MOTHER GOOSE (*wailing*). Ow-OW !
PETER. Mutton dressed as lamb, that's all ! She tricked me in this light—for a moment.
MOTHER GOOSE. Tricked you, did I ? (*Advancing on him.*) I'll do worse than that, you—you—ugly old woman, am I ? Silly old geezer, am I ? Stupid old hay-bag, am I ?
PETER. Y-yes !
MOTHER GOOSE. Jack ! Aren't I young and beautiful ? I yam, aren't I ?
JACK. Don't be silly, Mother ! And where's Ermyntrude ?

(MOTHER GOOSE *shrieks*.)

MOTHER GOOSE (*aghast*). Ermyntrude ! I'd forgotten her ! She was here a moment ago ! Them ghosts ! Them demons ! NO ! Them *bailiffs* ! Or was it ? Ermyntrude !
PETER. That's who we're looking for !
JACK. *I* only gave away an egg ! *You've* lost the whole goose !

(MOTHER GOOSE *collapses to* R.C. *They run and catch her. The* FAIRY SUNBEAM *enters on the bank, up* L.C., *in a pool of golden light.*)

FAIRY SUNBEAM.
Ah, Mother Goose, through vanity and pride
The Golden Goose might even now have died,
For wicked men have got her in their power
And none but I can save her in this hour.
And now, because you listened to temptation
You must return to your poor humble station.

(BLACK OUT. *The* FAIRY *vanishes.* LIGHTING UP. *The*
DEMON KING *appears on the Wishing Stone. He shrieks
at them. All the* DEMONS *rush on up* C., *to music, and
howls of laughter.* MOTHER GOOSE, PETER, *and* JACK
run off down R., *screaming.*)

(*Lightning.   Thunder.*)

No. 15a.   DEMON BALLET   ..   (*Music as in* No. 14)

(*As the* DEMONS *eventually dance down stage, the* TABS
CLOSE *behind them.*)

In front of TABS, *during scene change :—*

Complete DEMON BALLET, *if desired, with* SONG *by* DEMON
KING, *and* CHORUS *of* DEMONS.

SCENE 3.

SCENE.—*Outside* MOTHER GOOSE'S *cottage. As in Act* I, *Scene* I.

When the CURTAIN *rises,* SUSIE *is at* C., *surrounded by* VILLAGERS *and* MILKMAIDS. *They are singing :—*

No. 16.   SONG   ..   ..   .. (SUSIE *and* CHORUS)

(ALL *sing one refrain. Then* SUSIE *sings verse. Repeat refrain, and* DANCE *if desired.*)

After Number :—

(SAM *enters* R., *excitedly. Re-grouping.* SUSIE *at* R.C.)

SAM.   I say ! Have you heard the news ?
SUSIE.   No—what is it ?
SAM (*dramatically*). The Golden Goose has been stolen !

(*There are cries of dismay.*)

SAM.   It's true ! So Mother Goose is poor again, just as she used to be.
SUSIE.   Poor Jack and Jill !
SAM.   Poor goose, too ! They say it's all Mother Goose's fault. She got that stuck up and vain—and careless—and when she wasn't looking . . .

(*He sees* JACK *and* PETER *enter from the cottage.*)

Here is Jack—he can tell us.
SUSIE.   Oh, what happened, Jack ?
JACK.   I don't know—except that the goose has been stolen, we've no more golden eggs—we're as poor as ever, and that is all there is to it. (*He moves* L.C. *and sits.*)
CHORUS (*ad. lib.*). What a shame—someone ought to catch the thief—let's go and look for her (*etc.*).
SAM.   That's an idea ! Let's go and look for her—come on, you folk !

42

(*Exeunt* CHORUS *chattering.* PETER *is left at* C., *looking down at* JACK.)

PETER. I'm pretty sure I know who's behind this, Jack. (*He moves to* L.C.)

JACK. What d'you mean ?

PETER (*meaningly*). I wouldn't trust the Squire and those two ruffians of his further than I could see them. Don't forget he swindled you out of the very first egg.

JACK (*rising ; angrily*). It's all mother's fault, anyway ! She's been so different since we were rich. The money has just turned her head.

PETER. I know ! She doesn't like me because I'm a ploughman and not good enough for Jill.

JACK. And Betty, if you please, is not good enough for me. (*In ecstasy.*) That dear, sweet, little girl—that lovely little morsel—that altogether splendiferous . . .

PETER. I know—I know—I know ! What we've got to do is to win Mother Goose over to our side, and we can best do that . . . (*He breaks off, glancing* R.)

MOTHER GOOSE (*off* R.). Ermyn*trude* ! Ermy ! *Ermy* ! ERMY !

JACK (*crossing to* R.C.). She's not there, Mother ! I've called her till I'm hoarse !

(MOTHER GOOSE *enters* R.)

MOTHER GOOSE. Who said anything about a horse ? I want a goose ! (*Crossing to* C., *looking at the cottage.*) I could have sworn that was a castle last night. (*Holding her head.*) It must have been the salmon.

PETER (L.C.). Have you forgotten what happened in the forest last night ?

MOTHER GOOSE (*singing*). Down in the forest something stirred—it was only the voice of my GOOSE . . .

JACK. Be quiet, mother !

(JILL *hurries in* L. *followed by* BETTY.)

JILL. Have you found her ?

PETER. Not a sign !

JILL. Oh, dear ! (*She starts to weep.*)

(BETTY *runs across to* JACK.)

BETTY.   Oh, Jack !

PETER (*putting his arm round* JILL).   The best thing we can do is to get married—you will at least have enough to eat.

JACK (*at* R.).   Yes, and I'll marry Betty and go abroad ! (*He puts his arm round* BETTY.)

MOTHER GOOSE.   There'll be no marrying in this family till that Goose is found !

THE OTHERS (*in chorus*).   Well—where *is* our Goose ?

No. 17.   QUINTETTE.   " OH, WHERE'S OUR GOOSE "
                    (JACK, JILL, BETTY, MOTHER GOOSE, PETER.)

(Air : " *Begone, Dull Care.*")

ALL.   Oh, where's our goose ?
            Wherever can Ermyntrude be ?
            Oh, where's our goose ?
MOTHER GOOSE.
            She will not come back to me !
JILL.   So long have I been searching here—
BETTY.   From home they have cruelly torn her,
ALL.   We've been to look
            In every nook and corner.

ALL (*fortissimo, burlesqued à la Choral Society*).

Oh, where's our goose—(MOTHER GOOSE. Our goose !)
Wherever on earth can she be ? (MOTHER GOOSE. She
            be !)
Oh, where's our goose (MOTHER GOOSE. Our goose !)
Oh, bother and riddle-me-ree (MOTHER GOOSE. Me ree!)
If she has flown across the main
Her golden eggs to squander . . .

(CYMBALS CLASH.   *All stop.*   FAIRY SUNBEAM *appears up* L.,
        and moves a little down L.C.   *Others re-group.*)

FAIRY SUNBEAM.
            Stop singing ! For 'tis all in vain !
            The Magic Goose has gone again.
            Her gold caused only greed and vice,
            And all the sins of avarice !
            Sir Jasper has her in his power . . .

(ALL *react.*)

    She's locked up in his highest tower !
JACK.   Sir Jasper ! Then you were right, Peter !
MOTHER GOOSE.   The dirty dog !
JILL.   Oh, Fairy Sunbeam, can't you do anything ?
FAIRY SUNBEAM.   I will aid any mortal brave enough
to go to her rescue.
PETER. *I* will go ! I'm not afraid of the Squire and his
gang !
BETTY.   And Jack will go with you—won't you, Jack ?
JACK.   Of-of-of-co-course !
FAIRY SUNBEAM.

    Well said, young men ! You're true and brave !
    I'll show you how the goose to save.
    You must not storm Sir Jasper's tower
    Or he will kill her, in that hour.
MOTHER GOOSE.   Then what's to do, lass ?
FAIRY SUNBEAM.

    They must go to the Land of Geese
    And ask King Gander's help, for these
    Are birds of wonderful prowess
    Who'll surely rescue their Princess !
    Farewell !

    (BLACK OUT. FAIRY *vanishes.* LIGHTS UP.)

MOTHER GOOSE. Now, where have I seen her before ?
Could it have been at the bottom of my garden ?
PETER.   The fairy's right ! (*He crosses up* C.) Those
rogues would kill Ermyntrude rather than give her up.
I'll go to the Land of Geese at once !
JILL (*rushing to him*). My brave Peter ! (*She kisses him.*)
BETTY (*embracing* JACK). My hero !
MOTHER GOOSE.   Hey ! Break away, there !
PETER (*taking no notice*). I will scale the highest moun-
tains, swim the deepest rivers, force my way through ice
and snow, to give you back your goose and make you
happy, again my darling !
MOTHER GOOSE. You'll want spiked boots, a swim suit,
water wings, a snow plough, a few pick-axes and pneu-
matic drills—apart from that you'll travel light, I suppose.

(PETER *and* JILL, JACK *and* BETTY, *still in embraces.*)

BETTY.   And I'll pack sandwiches and aspirins for my sweetie !
JACK.   In case I come on later, as reinforcements . . .
BETTY (*hugging him*).   Darling !
MOTHER GOOSE.   Time !

(*The couples ignore this.*)

Time and a half !

(*They break apart.*)

Are you going to rescue this goose or not ? She'll be sitting on a dish of sage and onions by the time *you* get there !
PETER (*grandly*).   Madam, I will fly through fire and tempest to do your bidding ! But—when I bring Ermyntrude back safe and sound, I'll claim my reward.
MOTHER GOOSE.   Reward ? Anything you like, dear boy ! I've several old suits of my husband's . . .
PETER.   All I want is—your daughter Jill.
JILL.   Oh, please say "yes", Mother !
JACK.   And that goes for me and Betty—seeing that I may be giving a little assistance—and it *is* my *goose* !
MOTHER GOOSE.   I can't very well say "no" can I—now that I'm poor and old, and ugly, and neglected . . . Boo-hoo ! (*Wails.*)

(*They all go to her with cries of comfort. Enter* SAM *and* SUSIE *and* VILLAGERS, R., *and other* VILLAGERS *at* L.)

SAM.   It's no use, Jack. We've searched the village and the country-side—we've asked everyone.
JACK.   No matter ! We've just heard she's a prisoner in Sir Jasper's high tower, and Peter—and possibly myself ——is going to rescue her.
MOTHER GOOSE.   He's going all through the Weather Forecast to do it, too.
PETER (*modestly*).   I'm not really rescuing her myself.
JACK.   We've been advised to ask the help of the King of Goose Land.

JILL.   So he's off at once to the Land of Geese ! (*Tearfully*.) It's awfully d-dangerous !

SUSIE.   The Land of Geese ! That's miles away, right over the snow mountains !

MOTHER GOOSE.   Yes, and if someone doesn't get a move on, the Squire will get to hear of it and—(*with a neck-wringing gesture*) that will cook the goose !

SAM.   Then let's give Peter a good send-off !

SUSIE.   And Jack !

JACK.   Any time !   Any time !

No. 18.   CHORUS   ..   ..   ..   (THE COMPANY)

(*During the Number*, PETER *goes round shaking hands with everyone gaily*. JACK *goes round the opposite way, shaking hands limply. When they meet at* C., PETER *slaps* JACK *on the back*. JACK *nearly collapses, and continues his handshaking to* L., *while* PETER *continues to* R. *Finish the Number with stage picture*, PETER *at* C., *and* JACK *on his* L. *Characteristic bus, for each*.)

CURTAIN.

ACT III.

SCENE I.

SCENE.—*The Forest.*

As the CURTAIN *rises,* PETER *enters up* C. *to music, which ceases as he commences his first speech. He is dressed for mountaineering and carries a sword.*

PETER (*musing*). Well, this is the first stage of the adventure. This is where Ermyntrude was first lost and I must find my way to the Land of Geese from here. I must beg their help, restore Mother Goose's fortunes, and then—to claim my bride !

No. 19. SONG   ..   ..   (PETER)

(*After the Number* PETER *looks off* L., *shading his eyes with his hands.*)

Yonder lie the great snow mountains of the north—grim and forbidding !· I wonder what is on the other side ? (*He braces his shoulders valiantly.*) Well, I'm ready to dare anything to win my beautiful Jill, so on with the search !

(*He exits* L. *singing the refrain of the song.*)

(*Wind and thunder.*)

(JILL *enters* R. *stealthily. She is dressed in a cloak and hood and looks about her rather fearfully.*)

JILL. He went this way—I'm sure he did ! Oh, I couldn't let him go alone—I just couldn't ! (*Looking off* L.) Oh, there he goes—he's getting near the mountain pass now. I must hurry or I shall lose sight of him.

(*She moves* L., *but turns as* JACK *and* BETTY *enter hand in hand,* C. *They are muffled up in cloaks and furs and* JACK *wears a ridiculous fur cap and carries skis.*)

BETTY. Jill ! What are you doing here ?

JACK. You shouldn't come to the forest alone. It's full of ghosts and goblins who lead you astray and leave you to die . . .

(OWL *hoots.* JACK *staggers.*)

OW !

JILL (*contemptuously*). I don't care about goblins or ghosts. I'm going to follow Peter.

BETTY. He won't like that, Jill. He'll be afraid for you. You'd better go home.

JILL. I won't go back ! Why should Peter be the only one to face the dangerous snow mountains ?

JACK (*airily*). He won't ! Why do you think we're got up like a couple of Polar bears ? Do you think we're off for a day to (*local place name*). We've decided to go ourselves after all !

JILL. Oh, *have* you ?

BETTY. Yes, we're going. (*Hugging* JACK'S *arm tighter.*) Your Peter's not the only brave one.

(JACK *struts about with pride and trips down* R.C. *over his skis.*)

JILL (L.C.). Well, there's nothing in that. It's Jack's goose, after all.

BETTY (*indignantly*). Well, of all the ungrateful . . .

JACK (*holding up his hand in a dignified manner*). A-ah-ah-ah ! No quarrelling over *me*, girls ! I know I must look too, too utterly alluring in this outfit, but I beg of you to keep your heads—keep your heads !

JILL (*tartly*). I shan't have any difficulty in doing that —unless I laugh it off !

(*There is a sound of yodelling off, and* MOTHER GOOSE *is slowly drawn in on a toboggan up* C. *She is dressed in full "mountaineering" kit, and wears cycling breeches below the knee, striped stockings, enormous boots, a vividly embroidered waistcoat and an Alpine hat with a long feather in it. She carries an alpenstock and a hot water bottle, and on her back is an enormous rucksack with large spiked boots protruding from it*).

MOTHER GOOSE (*as she is drawn on*). Here we come, Mum, Dad's behind ! Any more for the funicu*lar* ? Yipee-ee ! (*She falls down the bank and picks herself up.*) First stop Clapham Junction ! (*Or local station.*)

No. 20. SOLO   ..   ..   ..   (MOTHER GOOSE

(*To be sung to the Chorus of "Off to Philadelphia."*)

Oh, I'm off on high adventure
To the land where geese are lent yer
And lay the rent for breakfast every morning ;
So I've packed me little rucksack,
And I don't expect to come back,
'Cos I've left me goods and chattels for the pawning.

JACK (*in despair*).   This is the end !
MOTHER GOOSE.   No, it's not, we haven't even started yet. (*Drawing up her toboggan.*) Jump up behind. (*She blows a whistle.*)
JILL.   You mean you're going on *that* ?
MOTHER GOOSE.   Certainly ! Up the Pole and down again—cheap day return one-and-fourpence—the only means of transport that hasn't been nationalised and therefore shows a profit . . . (*Waving her arms excitedly.*) We're off !

(*She falls off backwards. The contents of her rucksack fall out disclosing scarlet bedroom slippers, sponge-bag, scrubbing brush, mouth organ, sponge, etc., etc. The others help to pick these up as dialogue continues.*)

JACK.   What *are* you doing, mother ?
MOTHER GOOSE.   Doing ? Practising for the Olympic Games—can't you see ? Don't be silly ! I'm following Peter to the Land of Geese !
JILL.   So am I !
MOTHER GOOSE.   Oh, no, you're not !
JILL.   Oh, yes I am !
BETTY.   And so am I !

(MOTHER GOOSE *reacts.*)

JACK.   And so am I ! He'll need a man to help him.
MOTHER GOOSE.   I don't see the connection.   (*She heaves the rucksack into the toboggan.*)   However, if you must, you must !   But I refuse to go until I've sung a song. It's so good for travel sickness.   Join in the chorus if you like—I can take it !

(JACK, JILL, BETTY, *in bored attitudes, on toboggan.*)

No. 21.   SONG   ..   ..   ..   (MOTHER GOOSE)

(*After Number : Enter* SAM, SUSIE *and* VILLAGERS.)

JACK.   That's torn it !   Here comes the crowd now !
SAM.   Hullo, there !   What news of Peter ?
JILL.   We don't know.   Jack and Betty and I are going after him in case he needs help.   Come on, you two—I'm off !

(*She runs up the bank, jumps down and disappears, followed by* BETTY *and* JACK *in the same way.*)

MOTHER GOOSE.   Oy !   Wait for me !   Wait for me !

(*She piles into the toboggan, helped by the* VILLAGERS.   *Her luggage falls out, and is piled in again amid laughter. The toboggan is drawn up the bank.   She falls out backwards.   Bus.   The empty toboggan is drawn out of sight, and she runs off after it, screaming and shouting.*)

During the above, and after she has gone, the CHORUS *cheer and wave off, singing :—*

No. 22. FAREWELL CHORUS (SAM, SUSIE *and* VILLAGERS)

Close running TABS.

c

INTERLUDE.

In Front of TABS *during Scene Change.*
The entrance to the mountain pass.

PETER *enters* R. *singing No.* 22a *Reprise Refrain No.* 19.

At the close of this, the scene darkens, there is a flash and a rumble and the DEMON KING *appears in a subdued light. He is standing in a dramatic attitude with sword outstretched.*

DEMON.   Stay! Come nearer if you dare !
     I guard these mountains, so beware,
     Rash mortal ! If you still defy
     My warning you shall surely die.

PETER : Who are you to forbid me entrance to the Land of Geese ? I come to see King Gander and I'll trouble you to let me pass.

DEMON *(laughing fiendishly).*
     I am the guardian of the pass,
     And all who come this way must ask
     My sanction e'er they further go
     Into the silent Land of Snow.

PETER. I don't believe you ! You've no authority to keep me out. For the last time—stand aside, I say, and let me through, or it will be the worse for you.

DEMON.   Away ! I'll never let you through !
     Turn back, I say, before this day you rue !

(Brandishes his sword menacingly and PETER *draws his and raises it.)*

PETER. All right—you've asked for it. Guard !

(Spirited music as they go into a duel which lasts for a few moments. Suddenly, with a lightning thrust from PETER, *the* DEMON *falls dead.* PETER *stands over him triumphantly.)*

PETER. So perish all evil spirits and all who bar my way! He'll trouble us no more. Now the way lies open to the Land of Geese and the rescue of Ermyntrude. *(He looks off and upwards.)* I have only to scale that high mountain and the prize is mine. Hooray !

(He goes into Reprise of Song No. 22a *again and exits* L.)

CURTAIN.

SCENE 2.

SCENE.—*The Land of Geese.*

There is a background of snow mountains and icicles. At the back, C., KING GANDER *and* QUEEN KARIN *are seated on thrones. Around them is the* KING'S BODY-GUARD *of* GEESE *in military array. Grouped* R. *and* L. *are numerous* GEESE *of the* COURT.

No. 23.　CHORUS OF HOMAGE　..　　..　　(GEESE)

(To be sung to the tune of " Song of the Western Men.")

GEESE.　　We greet you now, your Majesty,
　　　　　Your loyal subjects true,
　　　　　We offer heartfelt loyalty,
　　　　　Your bidding fly to do.
　　　　　And if you should upon us call,
　　　　　Command us do or die,
　　　　　We'll rally round you one and all
　　　　　And never reason why.
　　　　　We greet you now, your Majesty,
　　　　　Your loyal subjects true,
　　　　　We offer heartfelt loyalty,
　　　　　Your bidding fly to do.

　　　　　May Fortune smile upon this realm
　　　　　And all who dwell therein,
　　　　　With good King Gander at the helm
　　　　　And lovely Queen Karin.
　　　　　May health and wealth upon thee shine
　　　　　Like sunbeams every day,
　　　　　Prosperity shall c'er be thine
　　　　　And love shall smooth thy way.
　　　　　We greet you now, your Majesty,
　　　　　Your loyal subjects true,
　　　　　We offer heartfelt loyalty,
　　　　　Your bidding fly to do.

53

KING (*graciously*). Thank you, thank you, my loyal subjects. Very nice ! (*Turning to* QUEEN.) Where are the children this morning, my dear ? Why have they not come in ?

QUEEN. I expect they're still looking for the early worms, dear. (*To a* GOOSE L.) Fetch them, Gracie.

(GRACIE *goes to wings* L. *and makes loud clucking noises. Enter several little* GOSLINGS R. *and* L. *They make obeisance to the* KING *and* QUEEN.)

NO. 24. BALLET   ..   ..   (GOSLINGS)

At the end of this the KING *and* QUEEN *and all the* COURT *applaud.)*

KING. Bravo, little goslings. You are learning to dance nicely. I hope you're learning your lessons just as well. Now run along and play a little longer in the snow.

QUEEN. But be sure and put your ear muffs on.

(*The* GOSLINGS *bow again and exeunt* R. *and* L. *dancing off to the same music. Enter a* GOOSE CHAMBERLAIN R., *who bows low to the* KING.)

CHAMBERLAIN. Your Majesty, there is a man at the Palace gates who says he wishes to see you on urgent business.

COURTIERS. A *man* ?

(*Fluttering among the* GEESE.)

QUEEN. Oh dear, I must powder my beak.

KING. What can a man want in the Land of Geese ? Show him in and we shall see.

(*The* GOOSE *exits* R. *and a moment later re-enters with* PETER. PETER *goes to the thrones and bows low.*)

PETER. Your Majesties, I come from Ptomania. I crave help from you.

KING. How can geese help men—the all-powerful and terrible ?

QUEEN (*nervously*). I have heard that men—er—sometimes—er—cook us !

KING. My dear—please—*please* !
PETER. Nevertheless, we cannot do without your aid now. Ermyntrude, our goose that laid the golden eggs, has been stolen by the wicked Squire, Sir Jasper Jabberwock.
KING (*in great concern*). Ermyntrude ? Our Princess Ermyntrude ?

(*The* COURTIERS *all murmur in quacks, with horror.*)

QUEEN (*quickly*). Is she safe ? Tell me quickly, before I swoon.
PETER. Yes, but she is shut up in a high tower. We dare not go to her rescue for fear the Squire kills her. He is greedy for her golden eggs and there is no knowing what he might do. The good Fairy Sunbeam sent me to you for help.

(*The* QUEEN *leans back faintly and* GRACIE *fans her with a large feather.*)

KING. She did quite right. We must lose no time in going to the rescue. (*Calling.*) Sergeant Gregory !

(GREGORY, *one of the* BODYGUARD, *steps forward smartly and salutes.*)

GREGORY. Sire ?
KING. Take a company of your most fearless ganders and fly quickly to Sir Jasper Jabberwock's castle. The Princess Ermyntrude is imprisoned in the highest tower there. Rescue her and bring her back to me. Arrest the Squire and his men also. They shall be made to pay for this !
QUEEN. Oh, how much shall we charge them, dear ? Enough to buy me a new hat ?
KING (*to* QUEEN). Be quiet ! (*To* GREGORY.) Sergeant Gregory ! Obey my orders !
GREGORY. It shall be done, sire. (*He salutes smartly, then turns and roars a few unintelligible orders. The* BODYGUARD *step forward smartly in formation and "goose-step" down* C.)

No. 25. "THE FIGHTING GANDOLIERS" .. (BODYGUARD
OF GEESE)

(To be sung to the tune of "The British Grenadiers.")

GEESE.   His Majesty, King Gander
          A soldier brave and true
          Has armies strong and loyal
          His bidding swift to do.
          But of all these hardy warriors
          None can with us compare,
          With a quack-quack-quack, we never turn back
          We're the Fighting Gandoliers!

KING, QUEEN *and* COURTIERS.
          With a quack-quack-quack, they never turn back
          They're the Fighting Gandoliers!

GEESE.   On pinions swift and silent
          We swoop upon the foe !
          As high o'er sea and mountain
          Our winged forces go.
          Each one a Fighting Gander
          And naught he will not dare,
          So a pat on the back and a quack-quack-quack
          For the Fighting Gandoliers.

KING, QUEEN *and* COURTIERS.
          So a pat on the back and a quack-quack-quack
          For the Fighting Gandoliers!

(March and counter-march—exeunt R., *goose-stepping. They
are followed by the* COURTIERS *who all join in the song
which gradually dies away as they exeunt.* PETER *watches
them go.)*

PETER *(longingly).* How I wish I might go with them !
KING *(kindly).* It is better not. You have no wings
and they will fly very swiftly and silently over the mountain
tops. They w.ll get to the tower long before you could
scramble down the mountain side.

QUEEN. Besides, you mustn't interfere with Gregory.
He's a bit touchy if you do.

(There is a whirring noise off.)

PETER.   Hark ! What is that ?
KING (*proudly*).   It is my geese taking wing. **Look !**
(*He leads* PETER R. *and points upwards.*) There they go in
fine arrowhead formation—the pride of my fighting force !
QUEEN.   My eldest boy is a Leading Aircraftgoose !

(*The whirring noise increases then gradually dies down.*)

PETER (*in awe*).   A wonderful sight indeed, your Majesty.
KING.   They will swoop on the tower and release
Ermyntrude before those ruffians realize they are there.
(*He struts* L.C. *proudly.*) Perhaps they will learn not to
insult a royal goose in future.
QUEEN.   Oh, I expect Ermyntrude would peck her way
out of anything, if I know her.
KING.   It's a pity Ermyntrude left home, but she was
always one for travel and adventure.
QUEEN.   She was a real problem child—always flighty
even when she was a little gosling.

(*The* GOOSE CHAMBERLAIN *enters* R.)

CHAMBERLAIN (*bawling*).   More visitors ! More horrible
humans !
(*Enter* MOTHER GOOSE, JILL, JACK *and* BETTY R. *They
come in very diffidently and look about them curiously.*)
KING.   Well, well, well, well ! We are honoured to-day.
QUEEN (*peering*). What are they—animal, vegetable, or
mineral ?
JILL (*seeing* PETER *and rushing to his side*). Peter—
darling ! You're safe ! (*They embrace.*)
KING.   What peculiar behaviour !
PETER.   Of course I'm safe. I only had one fight with
an awkward little demon on the Pass but I soon disposed
of him. You're forgetting your manners, darling. This is
King Gander and Queen Karin. They're helping us to
find the golden goose.
JILL.   Oh ! (*She curtseys.*) Your pardon, your Majesties.
QUEEN.   Granted, I'm sure.
PETER.   Your Majesties, here are Mother Goose, Jill
Goose, Jack Goose, and Betty Goose-girl.

QUEEN. Oh, my gooseness !

(*The* KING *and* QUEEN *move down and move about bowing
to each.* JACK *bows awkwardly and* BETTY *curtseys.*
MOTHER GOOSE *tries to curtsey and trips over her alpenstock.*)

MOTHER GOOSE. Whoops-a-daisy—over she goes !
BETTY. Oh, Mother Goose, do try and behave.
JACK. Yes, remember we're in Court, Mother.
MOTHER GOOSE. We're certainly up before the Beaks !
KING. You certainly aren't up before us—we're very
early risers. (*He looks at* MOTHER GOOSE *with interest.*)
So this is the famous Mother Goose ! Welcome to the
Land of Geese, madam. I've heard much of your kindness
to my subjects.
QUEEN (*crossing to* MOTHER GOOSE). Are you one of
the Gooses of Little Basting ?
MOTHER. GOOSE. No, one of the Ganders of Much
Frizzling.
KING. Very nice people, I've heard.
PETER. Mother Goose has always been kind to all
animals and birds.
MOTHER GOOSE. Hullo ! What do *you* want to borrow ?
KING. It was that heart of gold that earned you the
eggs of gold. The Princess Ermyntrude could not bear to
see one of our friends in need.
MOTHER GOOSE. Oh, bless her little heart ! So that
was why she turned her eggs into gold ?
QUEEN. She's like that—a bit impulsive. It's all or
nothing with her.
JILL. Please let her come back to us, King Gander.
JACK (*gloomily*). I don't suppose she'll want to come
now. You don't imagine she'd want to leave a posh home
like this for our cottage, do you ?
KING. We shall see—the Princess shall decide. And
now, while we are waiting for her, let me offer you some
refreshment.
QUEEN. Yes, you must be hungry and thirsty after
your long journey.
MOTHER GOOSE. Well, I must say I'm a bit peckish.

(JACK *nudges her.*)

O-o-oh ! Stop tickling !

QUEEN. The servants shall get you some nice, fresh *worms.* They are delicious, straight from the garden.

(*The others react, embarrassed.*)

MOTHER GOOSE. This is where this worm turns !

KING (*hopefully*). Or I can put you on to a new salad of water weeds.

MOTHER GOOSE. No, thanks, I prefer vinegar on mine.

JACK (*feebly*). I d-don't think I'm hungry.

PETER. I've *quite* lost *my* appetite !

BETTY. And please don't bother about *me* !

KING. No bother, I assure you.

JILL. I had breakfast just before I came out.

KING. Then perhaps the gentlemen will join me in a drink of pond water ? I have some that is well matured and has a very fragrant bouquet.

(MOTHER GOOSE *holds her nose.*)

PETER. Your Majesty is too kind. (*He makes frantic signs to the others to keep quiet.*) We appreciate your hospitality.

QUEEN. Oh, don't mention it !

KING. Any of Ermyntrude's friends are always welcome to lunch. (*To* JACK.) Now, what would you say to a couple of nice caterpillars ?

JACK. Oh—just, " Pleased to meet you " !

QUEEN (*to* MOTHER GOOSE). You will always find a seat on our perch and three good meals a day . . .

MOTHER GOOSE. I don't think I want full board—just bed and no breakfast !

(*The whirring of wings heard off. Excitement and re-grouping. The* KING *and* QUEEN *resume their thrones and the Goose family group around them. The* BODYGUARD *is heard singing. They enter,* R., *with* SIR JASPER, BERT *and* BILL.)

No .25a.　　REPRISE of No. 25 (2nd verse) .. (BODYGUARD)

After Number :—

F

Sgt. Gregory. The prisoners, Sire ! Caught red-handed, and just in time !

Mother Goose. A-ah ! You dirty gang of what-you-me-call-its !

Queen (*gasping theatrically*). Ermyntrude—what of that dear child ?

Jack (*anxiously*). Yes, where is she ?

Gregory. She is safe and well, your Majesty. She insisted upon preening her feathers before coming into your presence.

Queen. Oh—now I can swoon in peace !

(Gracie *goes and fans her.*)

Peter (*with great relief*). Oh, good work !

King (*sternly, to the prisoners*). And now, what have you to say for yourselves ? How dare you lay hands on a royal goose ?

Bill (*whining*). I never done it, Guv'nor. I wouldn't 'ave 'armed a feather of 'er 'ead, straight I wouldn't.

Bert. Besides, she kept us all at bay, 'issing and peckin'. Plucky little beggar, she is. (*He points at* Sir Jasper.) Ask '*im* where she pecked '*im* ! He can't sit down !

Queen (*triumphantly*). I knew she'd hold her own !

Sir Jasper (*furiously*). Why, you low-down, double-crossing blue-based baboons! (*He struggles to get at them, but is held back by* Geese.) I'll wring *your* necks instead of the goose's when I get at you !

Mother Goose. Naughty, naughty ! Nasty little temper !

Queen (*to* King). Oh, Ganny, did you hear that ? (*She goes to swoon again, but as* Gracie *is not looking thinks better of it.*)

King (*with deadly anger*). So *that's* what you intended to do ! Very well, you have condemned yourselves. (*To the* Sergeant.) Take them away, Gregory, and have them prepared for the oven, but *don't* wring their necks first.

(*The* Guards *close in and hold the prisoners.*)

Mother Goose. Try ringing their noses instead.

Queen. Gracie, *do* come here. I might want to swoon again.

JILL (*upset*).   Oh, poor men !
BETTY.   Perhaps they didn't mean it, after all.
PETER.   Be merciful, sire.
JACK.   Yes, wring their necks first.
KING (*unheeding*).   First make them mix their own stuffing, Gregory. (*To* SIR JASPER.) Let me see, you prefer sage and onions, don't you ?
SIR JASPER (*proudly and belligerently*). That's right—with apple sauce and thick gravy.
BILL (*dismally*). Washed down with champagne.
BERT (*hopefully*). Can we have the champagne first ?
KING. Enough !
BILL. We haven't had a drop yet !
KING. Away with them to the ovens and be sure to baste them well.
QUEEN. And don't leave the kitchen untidy.

(*The* GUARDS *are getting ready to march their prisoners out when* MOTHER GOOSE *steps forward. They hesitate.*)

MOTHER GOOSE. It's no use, I shall have to do something. I never could stand the smell of roast pork. (*To the* KING.) Your Majesty, please let them go this time. They are only fools, not villains.
SIR JASPER (*bridling*). How dare you call me a fool, woman ?
MOTHER GOOSE. And how dare you call me a woman, fool ?
KING. I dare not let them free, for the sake of others.
MOTHER GOOSE. I'll guarantee to keep them under control. Leave them to me !
KING. And how do you propose to do that ?
MOTHER GOOSE. Easy ! I'm going to marry Sir Jasper.
QUEEN (*peering at* SIR JASPER). Poor woman ! It must be her last chance.
JILL. You're *what* ?
BETTY. Surely not !
JACK. Mother, you can't !
PETER. Don't be too self-sacrificing, Mother Goose.
SIR JASPER (*taking one startled look at* MOTHER GOOSE *then speaking to the* KING.). I'm ready to be roasted alive, your Majesty. Lead on !

BILL.   'Ere, 'alf a mo' !   *We're* not !

BERT.   No fear !   You marry the old girl and give us a chance.

MOTHER GOOSE (*rolling up her sleeves*).   You leave it to me !   *I'll* keep 'em in order.

(*All laugh at* SIR JASPER, *while he glowers.*)

KING.   No, no, it won't do.   They deserve to die.

BILL *and* BERT.   Oh, *bother* !

KING (*politely*).   No bother at all—quite a simple matter.

QUEEN.   My husband arranges these things very well.

(*Soft music.   Enter* FAIRY SUNBEAM *and* ERMYNTRUDE R.)

FAIRY.   The Princess now returns in state,
     Her enemies are beaten,
     Brave Peter saved her from the fate
     Of being killed and eaten.
     The Demon Greed he fought and slew
     Because his love was good and true.

KING.   Welcome home, Ermyntrude.

QUEEN (*bursting into tears*).   Oh, Ermyntrude, I'm *so* happy !

KING (*to* PETER).   Choose what you will have for a reward, young man.

PETER.   Since Mother Goose wishes it, your Majesty, I would ask for the lives of these prisoners.

KING.   What ?   You really want to save them ?

JACK.   Yes, we all do.

(ERMYNTRUDE *goes to the* KING *and rubs her head against
him ingratiatingly.*)

FAIRY.   See, the Princess adds her pleas,
     I beg you, King, to grant them their release.

KING.   Very well, since you all wish it.   (*To the prisoners.*) You are granted a free pardon on condition that Mother Goose keeps you in order.

SIR JASPER.   That's a life sentence, not a pardon.

BILL.   Don't upset him again, Guv'nor.

BERT.   No, go easy with the sauce for the gander.

JILL *and* BETTY (*together*). Oh, thank you, your Majesty.

JACK. It's just as well not to have any ill feeling.

QUEEN. Well, I must say everyone's being very forgiving.

MOTHER GOOSE (*springing on* SIR JASPER *and throwing her arms round his neck.*) Jassy ! I've won you at last !

(BILL *and* BERT *back away, alarmed.*)

SIR JASPER. What do you take me for ? A prize in a sixpenny raffle ? (*He disengages himself.*)

MOTHER GOOSE. I think I'll throw a party when I get back.

KING (*gravely*). Where to, and who is the party ?

JACK (*miserably*). I suppose we'll have to say good-bye to Ermyntrude now.

MOTHER GOOSE. Oh dear, I can't bear to part with her. (*She gets out a huge handkerchief and sniffs.*) If only she'd come back with us I'd never bother about golden eggs again. She could lay addled ones for all I care. If I can have Ermyntrude to love I don't mind being poor —reely !

SIR JASPER. You speak for yourself.

(ERMYNTRUDE *goes and stands between* JACK *and* MOTHER GOOSE, *fondling them both. They stroke and pet her.*)

KING. She seems to be very fond of you.

QUEEN (*suddenly singing very loudly*). "Oh, sweet mystery of love . . ."

KING. Karin ! You forget yourself !

QUEEN. I'm sorry !

FAIRY (*to* MOTHER GOOSE).

    Well spoken ! By your words you've earned
    The right to have the goose returned.
    She shall go with you and remain
    To lay her golden eggs again.

SIR JASPER. Hooray ! I don't mind the bride chucked in with a dozen new-laid eggs.

MOTHER GOOSE. It's too good to be true ! We shall be able to have 18-carat omelettes for the rest of our lives !

KING.   She shall go with my blessing so long as her gold brings only happiness.

QUEEN (*tearfully*).   Yes, I suppose we ought not to stand in her light.

PETER.   Er—there's one more reward I want to claim from Mother Goose.

KING.   What's that, my boy ?

PETER.   She promised me the hand of her daughter if I should save the golden goose.

MOTHER GOOSE.   So I did. All right, she's all yours. You might as well have the rest of her with the hand.

JILL (*going to* PETER).   Peter—oh, Peter ! (*They embrace.*)

JACK.   Where do we come in ? What about Betty and me ?

MOTHER GOOSE.   You know your cues, don't you ? All right, you can get spliced, only don't say I didn't warn you.

(JACK *and* BETTY *embrace.*)

MOTHER GOOSE.   Any more ? I'm giving 'em away for old clo'es to-day.

SIR JASPER.   Well, you can change me for an aspidistra, if you like. (*He tries to sneak off but* MOTHER GOOSE *hauls him back by one ear.*)

KING (*chuckling appreciatively*).   I see you have the right touch, Mother Goose ! Is he the party you are going to throw ?

MOTHER GOOSE.   Yes, he's still got plenty of bounce.

BERT (*gloomily*).   I always told the Guv'nor he'd go too far one of these days.

FAIRY.   This is indeed a happy day
      When love at last is in full sway,
      Let marriage bells now gaily ring,
      And let us all be glad and sing.

(*Enter the Chorus of* GEESE *and little* GOSLINGS.)

No. 26.   CHORUS   ..   ..   (FULL COMPANY)

CURTAIN.

Scene 3.

Scene.—*A Room in* Mother Goose's *castle (as in Act* **2**, *Scene* 1.)

The scene is gay with flowers and decorations. On the rise of the Curtain *the* Villagers *and* Milkmaids *are in small groups, chatting animatedly. All are dressed in wedding clothes.*

No. 27. Opening Chorus *and* Dance. (Wedding Guests)

Susie. Oh, I feel so excited. I *do* love a wedding !
Sam (*laughing*). *A* wedding ! There are going to be three here today.
A Guest. *Three ?* (*Excited squeals from the others.*)
Sam. Yes, Mother Goose is making a family affair of it.
Susie (*dancing round*). Oh, how lovely. That means B tty and Jill are going to marry Jack and Peter at last.
Sam. And don't forget Mother Goose is marrying Sir Jasper as well.

(*Roars of delighted laughter from the others.*)

She's hardly let him out of her sight while she's been making preparations.
Susie. Well, I hope he'll turn over a new leaf and make her happy.
All. Hear ! Hear !
Sam. She'll make him turn over several new leaves before she's done with him.
Susie. And in a few weeks Sam and I are going to get married. I feel so excited I must sing.
Sam. Come on, then, let's all sing and dance. A wedding is a time for merrymaking !

A Reprise *of* No. 27.

No. 27a. Chorus and Dance .. (Wedding Guests.)

65

(At the end of this the GUESTS *group themselves and the music changes to a soft, "dreamy" tempo as* FAIRY SUNBEAM *enters* C. *and flits lightly down the steps.)*

FAIRY.   This is the day for which we've longed,
When all those mortals who've been wronged
Shall find true happiness at last
Now all their trials and storms are past.
The magic goose comes back to stay,
Once more her golden eggs she'll lay,
And Mother Goose and family
Shall never more know poverty,
So now—let wedding bells ring out
And greet the brides with joyful shout !

(She takes her place down L. *and the music changes to the Fighting Song of the Geese as* KING GANDER *and* QUEEN KARIN *appear on the top step* C. *and pause a moment before making a majestic entry. They are followed immediately by the* BODYGUARD *of* GEESE, *the* GOSLINGS *and several* GEESE *of the* COURT. *They group* R. *and* L. *The music changes as* BILL *and* BERT *enter, bowing* R. *and* L. *as they come down the steps. Comic bus. as they take their places among the girls.*

Appropriate wedding music as BETTY *enters on the arm of* JACK. *She is dressed as a bride and he is resplendent in very gaudy clothes. They are followed by* PETER *and* JILL *in the same manner. They group* R. *and* L.

Enter MOTHER GOOSE. *She is dressed as a bride but very exaggerated. She sparkles with "diamonds" and jewels. She leans "girlishly" on the arm of* SIR JASPER *and the two pose on the top step for a few moments while the* GUESTS *cheer, then they slowly descend and come down* C. *bowing graciously* R. *and* L. *until* MOTHER GOOSE *trips over her train and falls into the arms of* SIR JASPER, *who groans and staggers as he tries to support her.)*

MOTHER GOOSE.   Oh, what it is to have a man to lean on at last ! *(She leans heavily and* SIR JASPER *nearly lets her down.)*

Sir Jasper. Be sure your shins will find you out !

Mother Goose. You've no idea how nervous I feel—all of a twitter and flutter. (*She giggles and pokes* Sir Jasper *archly. To the* Guests.) Well, girls and boys, I must say you've overwhelmed me with your greetings. As soon as all this excitement is over we're going to spend a nice quiet honeymoon on the river.

Sir Jasper. Do drop in when you're passing.

(*The special music for* Ermyntrude *strikes up and the* Golden Goose *appears poised on the top step. All look towards her as she very slowly descends and comes down* c. Mother Goose *and* Sir Jasper *make way for her. The music still plays softly as* Fairy Sunbeam *steps forward*.)

Fairy.   The time has come to say good-bye,
          Our pantomime has ended,
          The story all ends happily
          As always was intended.
          There's only one thing left **to do**
          To make it perfect for us,
          I'll resurrect the Demon too
          To join the final chorus.

(*She goes to the wings* l. *and leads on the* Demon King.)

Demon. Thanks, Fairy Sunbeam, you're a brick,
          I own I played a dirty trick,
          But being killed is not much fun
          So here's good luck to everyone !

No. 28. Finale Chorus   ..   (Full Company)

Curtain.

NOTES ON LIGHTING.

ACT I.

SCENES 1 and 2.

All circuits full. F.O.H. flood White and Straw.
Spot PRINCIPALS No. 36 Lavender, for Numbers.

NO CUES.

INTERLUDE.

To open : Floats and No. 1. Batten Amber and Blue.
Spot and follow GOOSE No. 3 Straw.

FAIRY No. 36 Lavender.

At cue : BLACK OUT. Two FLASHES. Bring up Blue
only in No. 1. Batten. Spot FAIRY and
GOOSE as before. Spot DEMON KING Green.

At cue : B.O. LIGHTNING FLASH. (*Demon exits.*) Bring
up opening lighting and spots as before.

SCENE 3.

To open : Floats and Battens No. 32 Blue.

Flood back-cloth No. 32 Blue.

Flood C. acting area No. 17 steel on entrance
of SIR JASPER.

ACT II.

SCENE 1.

All circuits full. F.O.H. flood White and No. 3 Straw.

Spot PRINCIPALS No. 36 Lavender for Numbers.

At cue : (ERMYNTRUDE *quacks.*) B.O. No. 16 Blue-Green spot on DEMON KING, and bring in Blue only in floats and battens.

At cue : (DEMON . . . youthful beauty yet.) B.O. FLASH. Bring up opening lighting full, No. 36 Lavender spot on FAIRY, to fade on exit, with light check.

FRONT OF TAB No. Floats and No. 1 Batten FULL. Spot as desired.

SCENE 2.

To open : As for Act I, Sc. 3.
Spot and follow Ballet No. 16 Blue-Green.

End of Ballet : F.O.H. No. 17 Steel as before.
Spot GHOSTS and DEMONS No. 17 Blue-Green.

At cue : (GHOST *raised.*) B.O. and FLASH. Lights up.

At cue : (SIR JASPER . . . safe and sound.) B.O. Flicker lights for bus. Lights up as before.

At cue : (MOTHER GOOSE . . . demons or no demons.) B.O. and flashes. Lights up.

At cue : No. 16 Steel spot on MOTHER GOOSE at Wishing Stone. Fade as she leaves the Stone.

At cue : (*Enter* FAIRY.) No. 51 Gold spot on FAIRY.

At cue : (FAIRY . . . to your humble station.) B.O. FAIRY exits. Lights up. Spot DEMON KING No. 16 Blue-Green.

Follow bus. with : Lightning flashes.

DEMON BALLET : Flood DEMONS No. 16 Blue-Green (or No. 16 and White flicker wheel.)

IN FRONT OF TABS : Same lighting on Ballet.

SCENE 3.

All circuits FULL : Flood white and No. 3 Straw.
Spot PRINCIPALS **No. 36 Lavender for Numbers.**

At cue : (*Cymbal clash.*) White spot on FAIRY. B.O.
on exit. Lights up.

ACT III.

SCENE 1.

To open : Floats and Battens, Blue and Amber full
Pink $\frac{1}{2}$.

F.O.H. flood No. 3 Straw.
Spot PRINCIPALS No. 36 for Numbers.
For Final Chorus, bring up all circuits FULL, and F.O.H.
No. 36 Lavender and No. 51 Gold.

INTERLUDE.

To open : Floats and No. 1 Batten Blue and Amber.

Spot PETER No. 17 Steel.

After Reprise : Check Ambers. Lightning FLASH. Spot
DEMON KING No. 16 Blue-Green. Fade on exit, and
bring in Ambers.

SCENE 2.

To open : All circuits full. F O.H. No. 7 Pink and
No. 51 Gold.

At cue: (*Enter* FAIRY.) Spot and follow FAIRY White.

SCENE 3.

To open : All circuits FULL. F.O.H. No. 36 Lavender
and No. 51 Gold.

No cues.

FURNITURE AND PROPERTIES.

ACT I.

SCENE 1.

Small wooden bench.
Tree stump.
Pump (*optional*).
Pails for MILKMAIDS.
MOTHER GOOSE : Broom.
SIR JASPER : Hunting crop.
Ready in cottage : Broken chair. Aspidistra. Old fur
  tippet.
Ready off R. : Golden egg.

SCENE 2.

Chicken house. Seat. Tree stump.
JACK : Bucket.
MOTHER GOOSE : Basket filled with broken crocks, for
  crash.
Golden egg in chicken house.
Ready off R. : Very large golden egg.

SCENE 3.

Wishing Stone. Log.

ACT II.

SCENE 1.

Two small settees. Two chairs. Palms, or pillars.
FLUNKEY : Tray with glasses of wine.

SCENE 2.

As before.

SCENE 3.

As before.

ACT III.

SCENE 1.

PETER : Rucksack, and sword.
JACK : Fur cap. Skis. Bundle.
MOTHER GOOSE : Rucksack. *In it :* Scarlet slippers,
large scrubbing brush, sponge bag, mouth organ, etc.
Alpenstock. Hot water bottle. Bundle.

SCENE 2.

Dais, and two thrones.
KING : Sceptre.
QUEEN : Smelling salts.
GRACIE : Fan.
BODYGUARD : Short sticks with feathers.

SCENE 3.

No special props. Furniture, etc., as before.

www.ingramcontent.com/pod-product-compliance
Ingram Content Group UK Ltd.
Pitfield, Milton Keynes, MK11 3LW, UK
UKHW021823150726
7214IPUK00017B/280